About Sanctuary

Greg Johnson knows the sacred stillness of the Great Smokies. If you can't get there yourself – to the summit of Thunderhead or the sunrise at Andrews Bald or the 360-degree spectacle from Mt. Cammerer – or if you just want to taste the memory once again, this is the book for you. Greg is a bona fide East Tennessean and Smoky Mountain lover and if you are not already one, his meditations will help make you one, too.

Lamar Alexander
Former Governor of Tennessee and U.S. Education Secretary

I love being outdoors and feel very fortunate to have grown up in East Tennessee with the Great Smoky Mountains right in my backyard. Like Greg, my wife Elizabeth was raised in Sevier County, and we couldn't be prouder that he's chosen to celebrate the Park's 75th anniversary in this meaningful way. .These mountains truly are a national treasure, and I hope its visitors continue to enjoy them as much as we do.

Bob Corker
U.S. Senator, Tennessee

Greg Johnson has lived his whole life in the foothills of the Great Smoky Mountains. He is descended from East Tennesseans who lived in those beautiful mountains. While he appreciates the economic benefits and enjoyment provided by the Park, he also understands the heartbreak and sacrifices of many very poor people whose land and farms were taken from them. No one could write about the Great Smoky Mountains and the Park with more talent, feeling and balanced understanding.

John J. Duncan, Jr.
U.S. Congressman, Tennessee's 2nd District

Greg Johnson's love for the Great Smoky Mountains is evident throughout this delightful book. He has captured the majesty of this glorious preserve as well as the individual passion it ignites in those fortunate to walk its trails. You cannot read Greg's book without wanting to get out your hiking stick and start up one of the Park's beautiful trails.

Jim Hart
President, Friends of Great Smoky Mountains National Park

Most people I know love the Great Smoky Mountains. My family's love for the Smokies and our relationship with the mountains go so deep, the Walker Sisters of Little Greenbrier always referred to my father as "Cousin J. B." Greg Johnson's "Sanctuary" offers an abundance of proof of how much God loves the Great Smoky Mountains. How else could the wonders of nature, the stillness of the wilderness and the serenity Greg describes exist?

John B. Waters, Jr.
Former Chairman of the Board, Tennessee Valley Authority

These ancient hills are familiar to East Tennesseans, but they become new in Greg Johnson's voice. Though millions pass through the National Park, here is a rare, original experience of the Smoky Mountains; a fresh, life-giving encounter won by patience and quiet contemplation of God's magnificent presence. Whether Greg climbed steep, rocky ascents, strolled along silent pathways, or rested by calm, mountain streams, I went with him every step of the way. In the end, I discovered he had taken me on two journeys: one across these ancient mountains, another into the story of his soul.

The Reverend Jack King
Assistant Vicar, Apostles Anglican Church, Knoxville, Tennessee

Greg Johnson welcomed me into his heart and mind as I served as his spiritual director. Now he welcomes you and me to what every human being needs – sanctuary, a place of grace. This wordsmith brings me back to hikes I have enjoyed in a manner that excites me to return and relive that sanctuary. I wish the same for you.

Reverend Arne Walker
Semi-retired pastor, ELCA, Gatlinburg, Tennessee

About Sanctuary

In 1990, Greg Johnson discovered the largest shoulder to cry on in the history of grief management. Struggling from the sting of divorce, he turned to the 521,600-acre Great Smoky Mountains National Park. Hiking the trails, listening to the patter of rain, feeling the wind and gazing from wilderness vistas, Johnson discovered an inner peace he thought was gone from his life forever.

As any introspective park visitor can attest, these mountains truly are a source of sanctuary. But rare is the trail walker who can capture this feeling and transform it into words as Johnson has done.

Johnson would have you believe he is not a naturalist, historian, geologist or botanist. Not by collegiate degree, perhaps; but be not fooled. His descriptions of people and places in the Great Smokies are alive with detail only a trained eye could see.

He may not be a poet or theologian, either. But as these chapters unfold, you will discover Johnson's special talent for singing the praises of God's Creation. If you can't get religion from these experiences, you ain't payin' attention!

Sam Venable
Columnist, Knoxville (Tenn.) News Sentinel

Sanctuary

Meditations from the Great Smoky
Mountains National Park

J. Greg Johnson

Sanctuary: Meditations from the Great Smoky Mountains National Park

© 2009 J. Greg Johnson

Published by Flat Creek Publishing

Printed @ CreateSpace.com in the United States of America

All rights reserved. No part of this publication may be reproduced, stored in a retrieval system, or transmitted in any form or by any means, electronic, mechanical, photocopying, recording or otherwise, without the prior written permission of the author except for short excerpts or quotations for reviews.

ISBN: 1441455957

EAN - 13: 9781441455956

Cover photo: Alum Cave Trail near LeConte Lodge
Sunset photo at Clingmans Dome by Diane E. Johnson
All other photos by J. Greg Johnson

Dedication

To my father, who blazed the trail; my mother, who taught me to enjoy it; my wife, Diane, who has inspired me to climb higher than I ever dared; and my children, Micah, Haley and Reed, who have embarked upon paths of their own.

Acknowledgments

Special thanks to: Tim Line and his staff at LeConte Lodge for another amazing stay on the mountain; Bob Miller, Nancy Gray and Kent Cave, staffers at the Great Smoky Mountains National Park, who answered my often inane questions; Bruce Hartmann, Jack McElroy and Hoyt Canady at the Knoxville (Tenn.) News Sentinel, who took a chance that changed my life, and to my editor extraordinaire, Jan Maxwell Avent.

Contents

Foreword	1
Introduction	11
Andrews Bald	17
Clingmans Dome	23
Baskins Creek	29
Walker Sisters Cabin	35
Chimney Tops	41
Grotto Falls	47
The Jump Off	53
Charlies Bunion	57
Gregory Bald	63
Sugarlands Quiet Walkway	69
Little Greenbrier Schoolhouse	75
Ramsey Cascades	81
Rocky Top	87
Thunderhead Mountain	93
Spence Field	99
Mt. Collins Shelter	105
Newfound Gap	111
Rainbow Falls	117
Albright Grove	123
Mt. Cammerer	129
Abrams Falls	135
Cades Cove	141
Laurel Falls	147
Porters Creek	153
Mt. LeConte – Alum Cave Trail	159
Mt. LeConte – LeConte Lodge	165

Mt. LeConte – Myrtle Point	171
Mt. LeConte – Clifftops	177
Psalm of the Smokies	183
Finding Sanctuary	187
Sanctuary Rated	195

Foreword

I have known popular Gatlinburg architect Tom Trotter since the fourth grade. Some East Tennessee old-timers may remember that his mother and father brought the concept of "family style" restaurant service to Pigeon Forge in the late 1950s. Trotter's was a favorite gathering place for locals and tourists alike, and Tommy, as I still call him, was – and is – a dear friend. Shortly after he reached the age of forty, fully cognizant of his own mortality, he suggested that we, as native mountaineers, had the absolute obligation to "hike all of the trails in the Smokies" as a part of our "bucket list." Little then did we imagine the magnitude of our ambitions (twenty years later we are well short of our goal).

Soon thereafter, Tom planned a series of hikes, one of which led us to Mt. Cammerer along the Low Gap Trail out of the Cosby Campground trailhead. The trek was difficult, but the reward was spectacular. On one of those days that you could see forever, we got the full treatment – all three-hundred sixty degrees – from atop this rocky peak near the state boundary. Of course, Tom immediately recognized the architectural significance of the western style fire tower. Its condition was deplorable, however, and graffiti adorned the interior walls.

In the week following, Tom lodged a complaint with Great Smoky Mountains National Park Superintendent Randall Pope. When the superintendent explained that there was simply no money to restore the facility, Tom volunteered to donate the architectural services necessary, and, at the same time, assured Randy that his "friend Gary," who, he claimed, had a few fundraising experiences during his tenure as the Sevierville mayor, could help generate the necessary funds.

Randy telephoned me on that specific project, and I pledged to assist, but he had bigger plans. So, on September 3, 1993, Superintendent Pope called together a collection of Smokies' lovers from North Carolina and Tennessee to discuss the formation of a Park support group. There, I met for the first time a cast of wonderful people that by the end of the day had become the founding directors of Friends of the Great Smoky Mountains National Park. Among those in attendance were such notables as Lindsay Young, Natalie Haslam, Judy Morton, and Mary Johnson from Tennessee and, from North Carolina, Barney Coulter, Steve Woody, and John Dickson.

Randy and his sidekick, Park Management Assistant Bob Miller, the familiar "face and voice" of the Smokies, coordinated the meeting, explaining that the Park needed a way to raise "a little money" so as to address its backlog of capital needs – the Mt. Cammerer Fire Tower among them. Parenthetically, Randy retired four months later, but I credit him for opening the doors of the Park to private sector support. And Bob, who still serves as the administrative liaison, has not missed a single meeting of the Friends of the Smokies since its inception. In sum, some pretty nice things came from our hike in the Park.

If you have read this far, a fair question might be, "What has all of this got to do with Greg Johnson and 'Sanctuary'?" Well, never expect a short answer from anyone from the legal profession (In the words of Abe Lincoln; "A lawyer's time is his stock in trade."). I will try to explain, but I must digress.

If you live in the rural regions of Southern Appalachia, there is a good chance you have been there for a while. I plead guilty to being a product of several families who have resided in Sevier County for at least ten generations (counting my grandchildren). And, of course, you can hardly have a conversation with a real mountaineer without qualifying yourself as an Ogle, Whaley, Reagan, Ownby, Maples or Huskey, or at least explaining how you are related to one of those families. I qualify as "bona fide" on several counts (some of which are a bit embarrassing), but mostly because my dear mother, Kate, was a Reagan.

Her father, West, was born in the Sugarlands in the late 1800s and lived there until he found job opportunities in Knox County around 1915. He was 6th generation on the Reagan side, the first being Timothy, a Revolutionary War veteran who had been wounded in the Battle of Brandywine before moving to Sevier County in 1795. Grandfather's Irish ancestry (O'Riagan, according to the Reagan/O'Reagan genealogy) served him well when, as a young man, he farmed for subsistence in difficult circumstances.

Further, although my mother spent her formative years in South Knox County, she loved the mountains and came back home as soon as she finished her secondary education. She met and married my Dad, Dwight Sr., and helped persuade him to trade a new 1950 Ford for two acres on the Middle Prong of the Little Pigeon River just outside what had by then become the (Big) Greenbrier Park entrance. Dad built a cabin where my brothers and I spent much of our time – swimming, fishing, hiking, and camping – until each of us went away to school.

When I learned that my fellow Sevier Countian, Greg Johnson, whose life I have followed since he was a little tyke, had chosen to display his significant writing skills in a book designed to celebrate the 75th Anniversary of the Great Smoky Mountains National Park, I thought it was my natural duty to check out his "bona fides." First and foremost, Greg is a local boy, one of three sons of David and Dorothy Johnson.

Although "only" third generation Sevier County on the Johnson side, he goes back eight generations, by my count, through the

Ownbys of Big Greenbrier on his father's side. Although the Atchley and the Sims families (on his mother's side) were from the foothills rather than the mountains, that is close enough to suit me. The point, of course, is that Greg is not only an accomplished writer, having demonstrated his talents in a professional capacity as a freelance opinion columnist for the Knoxville News Sentinel, but he also qualifies as a genuine mountaineer!

In truth, of course, you don't really have to be from these parts to fully appreciate the serenity of the Smokies. Horace Kephart, author of "Our Southern Highlanders," left his position as library director in St. Louis in order to seek refuge in the Hazel Creek area of North Carolina. His writings helped make the case for our national park. George Masa, born Masahara Izuka, was a Japanese businessman before forever leaving his native country and then spending the last eighteen years of his life as a photographer in the Smokies. These talented and yet troubled men found sanctuary in the Smokies during the formative years of the Park. Today, they enjoy legendary status in the folklore of our most precious natural resource.

For the same reasons those two historic figures "got here as soon as they could" and made this their home, many of the mountain families in East Tennessee and Western North Carolina have chosen to stay in these lands. And, like so many others, Tom Trotter and I have found refuge along the trails and upon the mountaintops in the Smokies and have worked out a few of life's little problems along the way. A day with Mother Nature very often produces positive consequences.

In "Sanctuary," native son Greg Johnson pays tribute to the Smokies as his own spiritual retreat. So, as you figuratively join Greg on one of his favorite hikes, whether to Mt. Cammerer, Andrews Bald, or Spence Field, refresh your soul, as he has done, with the remedial qualities of our mountains and streams.

Through this compelling tale of the peaks and valleys in his personal life, Greg reminds us of the parallel between the inevitable ups and downs in our years on this Earth and the various changes of grade on the trail. In his words, "If you keep walking through the steep parts, you get to see the beauty." Life, indeed, is both the journey and the destination.

Gary R. Wade
Chair Emeritus
Friends of the Great Smoky Mountains National Park

Sanctuary

Great Smoky Mountains National Park

Sanctuary

Alum Cave Trail

The Beginning

Sanctuary

Great Smoky Mountains National Park

"I went to the woods because I wished to live deliberately, to front only the essential facts of life, and see if I could not learn what it had to teach, and not, when I came to die, discover that I had not lived."

Henry David Thoreau

"But, (Jesus) Himself often withdrew to the wilderness and prayed."

Luke 5:16 (New King James Version)

Sanctuary

Introduction

Near the top of the Great Smoky Mountains, on the western edge of the Clingmans Dome parking lot, stands an informational display that reads, "Mountains: Refuge and Healing." The marker recounts the sacredness of the Smokies to the Cherokees, the original inhabitants of this land. The plaque quotes naturalist John Muir: "Thousands of tired, nerve-shaken, over-civilized people are beginning to find that going to the mountains is going home." The display concludes, "What do these mountains mean to you?"

For me, the Great Smoky Mountains National Park may have saved my life. For sure, the blue-green backdrop for the masterpiece that is this part of God's Creation saved my sanity. Growing up in Sevier County, Tennessee, in the shadows of the Smokies, familiarity bred disregard as I hurried through life, intent on "making it," seldom taking time to take in the grandeur of our place, furiously pushing forward with hardly a glimpse up toward the high country.

Life hummed along grandly – childhood, high school, college, football coaching (a dream come true), marriage, a son, a new job that challenged me and paid me enough to build a nice house after my twins were born – until the divorce. Wracked by the pain that came from the dissolution of a dream, I turned to my faith, to my church, to my friends. All were helpful, yet healing was uneven and uncertain, my mind constantly consumed by my failure, my kids, my work and my pain. I went to the Downtown YMCA in Knoxville on my lunch break to exercise my body and exorcise the toxins of grief, anger and humiliation.

Feeling stronger physically if not psychologically, I made my way home from work one afternoon in the early 1990s, turned off Interstate 40 at the 407 Exit, headed south on Highway 66, crested the hill in Kodak and saw – really saw, perhaps, for the first time – the Smokies stretched out before me. My tension and turmoil eased.

As I drove on toward Sevierville, Mt. LeConte loomed ahead. As the road descended toward the French Broad River, I looked up at LeConte and said to myself, "I'm going to climb that mountain."

The next morning, a Saturday, I cinched up my athletic shoes, threw my Bible, a notebook, a ballpoint pen, a few snacks and some water in a backpack and hightailed it to the Great Smoky Mountains National Park. Crossing the bridge from the parking lot into the green tunnel of trees at the beginning of the Alum Cave Trail, I paused to let the symphony of the river wash over me. Anxious to get to the top, I hurried on, confident I was equipped for the path ahead.

It took less than half a mile to understand that riding stationary bikes, jogging on treadmills and pumping on stair-climbing machines in the air-conditioned Y bore absolutely no semblance to hiking in the Smokies. Another half-mile proved that soft-soled athletic shoes are no match for the ages-old rocks jutting up on the trail. Within another half mile, after the trail turned decidedly steeper, I was sucking wind.

I paused, drank some water, stretched, drank some more water and headed off toward the top. The trail didn't relent. I was off on an adventure for which I was totally unprepared. My breathing was so labored and my self-flagellation for my lack of physical conditioning and my naiveté about the mountains was so intense, I did not, could not enjoy the scenery. Again gasping for air, I played my hole card, resorted on my last resort, grasped for my last lifeline…

I prayed. Honestly, it wasn't a very pious prayer. Rather, it was a prayer of self-preservation. "Lord, help me make it up this mountain," I said. Or something close to that. The next phrases of the prayer are lost in time but, if I recall correctly, I made several bargains with God which I hope he doesn't remember because I sure don't.

Though the prayers started out pathetic, I noticed that I wasn't noticing my labored breathing quite so much. I noted aloud that the trail is a lot like life, some sections steep, others gentle, still others with roots and rocks as obstacles to be negotiated. Then, higher up the trail, at the first break in the green corridor that surrounded me, the vista of the valley burst into view. "Ahhh," I thought. "If you keep walking through the steep parts, you get to see the beauty."

I was hooked. I scampered on up the mountain, catching a second wind, inspired now by the challenge and scenery, praying along the way, entranced by the mystery of the mountains. I burst into the lodge on top of LeConte, wild-eyed and winded, my head as light as the mountaintop air, feeling a sense of accomplishment and sensing peace in my spirit for the first time in months. If I remember correctly, I walked up to Clifftops, gazed out toward Newfound Gap and felt the wind lift away the troubles I still carried from the mess of my life down below.

It was there, I think, that I first wrote a few notes about what I saw, what I was feeling, what I was experiencing. An athlete from birth, a jock for years and, then, a stockbroker by trade, reflection and contemplation had no place in my Type-A world. A journal was a newspaper from Wall Street, and meditation was something practiced by a yogi on an Asian mountaintop. In that moment, in that rarefied air, practicing an unfamiliar activity, life changed.

By the time I got back down to my car, I had begun to plot my next adventure. My brother Jeff taught me what he could about the mountains – I was so eager I barely listened – and I started buying equipment and maps and scheduling times to go to the woods. Over the next few years, I hiked the Appalachian Trail through the Smokies (an east to west adventure), hiked from Deep Creek in North Carolina to Gatlinburg (a south to north traverse), formed a hiking group at my church and took them on several day hikes and up to LeConte Lodge for an overnight, hiked with my twin daughters, climbed the

Chimneys with my son and kept coming back to the Smokies, sometimes in search of my sanity, other times just to walk in the woods.

My journal became my constant companion, a place to work out life and work on myself. I carried it into the mountains as well as overseas when I made mission trips to Russia and Kenya. It was no formal affair and there were long gaps between entries. But, writing began to fascinate me. I tried to describe sunrises and sunsets which inevitably led me to some sort of self-discovery. I tried to describe the wind – and am still trying – and I tried to communicate with my Maker and make sense of life.

As the 75th anniversary of the Great Smoky Mountains National Park approached, I thought often about my trips into the Smokies in those difficult days. My journeys into the mountains have been more sporadic over the past several years, with kids to raise and ballgames to attend and the flow of life whisking me away from the place I found peace.

Here, in this book, I travel back to some of the places I've been before to meditate on the mountains, to look at life in the here and now. As you'll discover, I'm no naturalist, I'm not a geologist, I'm no historian, nor am I a botanist. My view of the Great Smoky Mountains comes from my experiences there and the faint yet visceral knowledge that my paternal grandmother's people made their homes in Greenbrier back before the Park was formed.

There's another plaque in the Clingmans parking lot. It asks, "How did this land come to be?" This display tells the Cherokee version of Creation and has an excerpt from a geologist's point of view about the formation of the Smokies. It also contains a familiar quote from Genesis: "In the beginning, God created the heavens and the earth…" For me, these mountains, the Great Smoky Mountains, are a spiritual place, a gigantic chapel of refuge and healing, a sanctuary where I can worship in the wilderness and let God minister to me through His Creation.

As the Great Smoky Mountains National Park turns 75 in 2009, these words, these photos, these thoughts are my birthday blessing to the mountains, my eulogy for those who lived its history, tramped its backcountry and left their land so the land might be left for us to enjoy today. And this is my public thank-you to the public officials, the Park personnel and the private citizens who made this place, maintain this place and love it as much as I do.

I've several mountaintops left to explore, many more miles of trail to walk and much more to discover in the cathedrals of the Great Smoky Mountains. Come on – join me in the journey, venture inside this half-million acres of holy hills and find sanctuary in the Smokies.

Greg Johnson
Fall 2008

Sanctuary

Andrews Bald

I missed the sunrise. The bed's invisible straps held me almost half an hour too long, begging me to stay after a week of wear and a Friday afternoon from hell. I missed the sunrise, but I caught most of the magic hour, that time just after dawn when daybreak runs across the ridges and along the spine of the Smokies and nudges the mountains awake.

There's a gentleness in this hour, a soft caress of linear light that casts graceful shadows on the new day. The breeze this morning comes like a lover's kiss, tenderly stirring the senses, whispering away the slumber as it brings blood to the cheeks. Birds dart among the firs, dancing on the awakening winds, before diving off the side of the bald.

I need this place. With grasses waving between the rhododendron and spruce, with its panorama off into North Carolina, with its easy sun, I always find peace on Andrews. I'm alone on the bald so far and that's fine with me. More than fine actually – it's perfect. And by design. I left well before daybreak to beat the crowds. After a week of dealing with dollars and deadlines, phone calls and frustrations, here I can come and let nature nurture me, let the mountains minister to me, let the winds awaken the poet within me.

Up here, looking down on the clouds that creep through the tucks and folds of the Smokies, I am at once lifted high and laid low. I'm far removed from computer screens and handheld devices, e-mails and emergencies, the urgent and the irrational. As I step out of the trees and onto the bald, my world is suddenly larger, cleaner, greener. The air becomes noticeable, something to be sensed and savored, a delicacy rather than merely matter for consumption. Yes, I'm reminded of my Creator – The Creator – and I gawk again at His handiwork, amazed all over by the beauty of His Creation.

If my problems and projects and the details of life seem less significant here, I seem even less so. Standing on top of this part of the world, I sense my own smallness, my insignificance in the larger world, the Greater Scheme. Hundreds if not thousands have come before me to this place, many of whom came decades ago to graze cattle on this bald, and before that, the natives who hunted here for elk and deer so their families could live through winter. Yet, as small as I am in this moment, each brush of the breeze across my neck or on my cheek reminds me of God's love for me, His awareness of me, His alertness to the needs of me, one of his creations.

The mountains feel different at 50. As I drove up in the dark this morning, the stress and tension of a too-fast life drained as I wound toward the top. Tears welled in my eyes, tears of tension spilling over, tears of gratitude and gratefulness for the life I've been given, tears of thanksgiving for having made it through troubles and tears of relief at finally finding my soul at rest. Now, as I come to these mountains, I seek sanctuary, a place for my soul to be soothed and stirred, comforted and confronted, healed and inspired. It's not too trite, I don't think, to say I come to worship, to meet God in these mountains.

A smile crinkles as I remember a younger man on these mountains. Freshly divorced, determinedly driven, that 30-something me looked at these mountains and saw something to be climbed, a place to be conquered, a showcase for my vitality and a pedestal for my masculinity. "How far?" "How high?" "How fast?" marked most every trip. Even then, though, the poet appeared or at least the poet as I understand one to be – a soul so scarred or scared that he dares to look inside and stare, as Jean Val Jean sings in the stage version of Victor Hugo's "Les Miserables," into the void and even into the whirlpool of his sin, and then either quiveringly or courageously writing down his despair or determinedness or delight. As the 30-something me looked in, I found darkness and light, love and hate, joy and anguish, courage and absolute terror. Little was resolved back then, other than to keep walking, keep climbing, keep coming back to the majesty of the mountains.

I smile again as I recognize that the 50-year-old me still measures and marks and is still invigorated by these walks in the Smokies. I'm still determined, still driven but with a bit more balance. I hope. My desires now are to do good, to do well and to finish strong instead of to stack up accomplishments and accolades. But, yes, the mountains still release my manliness, at least for a while, as I regale in their ruggedness when I slop through the muck and heave myself over the rock-strewn trail.

A wren just hopped by, hunting for handouts, while his bigger cousins dance in the taller trees. I saw two bears on the drive up, each

sauntering across the road and disappearing into the woods before I could grab my camera. I hoped for deer here on the bald, but none were stirring. I arrived too late, I guess.

The sun has sneaked higher and is warming quickly. The long shadows of morning are almost unnoticeable now. I hear the wind rushing down the valley, carrying its caress to the west, circling back to my cheek to remind me it's here, He's here and so am I.

Sanctuary

"Everybody needs beauty as well as bread, places to play in and pray in where nature may heal and cheer and give strength to the body and soul."

John Muir

Clingmans Dome

Quiet has yet to come to the top of the Smokies. Families and couples are here on the Clingmans Dome tower. Some speculate about seeing Mt. Pigsah on a clear day. Others try to spot Gatlinburg in the distance. Still others wonder about the Appalachian Trail and ponder its almost imponderable 2000-plus miles.

The haze hangs low today and hangs on, not burned away by a summer sun that spiked the valley to almost 100 degrees, while the temperature hovers below 70 degrees here in the highlands. The sun sinks slowly, burning through the haze and the *shaconage* – the Cherokee word for the blue smoke that gives these mountains their name – giving life to this day for perhaps another half hour.

That's why we're here, the sunset. A group of photographers had staked claim to one of the pulloffs along the road back down the mountain, tripods ready to capture the grandeur of the end of a day. There's no way really, no matter the talent, no matter the technology, to seize the scenery or reproduce the reality of sunset in the Smokies. Not with a camera, nor with a brush, nor with a pen. The gentle decrease in temperature as day ends, the softness of the ever-present breeze, the smell of sunset, that slight shift in scent as day dies, elude even the most artistic among us.

Clingmans holds memories. On a hike along the Appalachian Trail through the Smokies years ago, Dad and my son, Reed, met me here, down below the tower, to resupply me and give me a Diet Coke and chocolate break at roughly the midpoint of those 75 miles. Dad looked relieved I was still alive, given his constant worry before I left that I was too green to go it alone. My son looked shocked and somewhat scared of his father, this wild man with a scraggly beard, unkempt hair, a bandana for a headband, splattered with mud and smelling of the woods after days on the trail. Even sharing Little Debbie cakes and soda didn't calm him much.

Color is coming to the end of the day. The blue deepens above as the sun sits on the haze out past the western end of the Park. Oranges and pinks rise below as the outlines of Silers Bald and Thunderhead Mountain and Gregory Bald darken to blue before turning to purple. The crowd on the tower has quieted, even the little ones, as if sensing something spectacular is about to occur.

We've all turned west, waiting, watching, snapping photos in hopes of a moment we can etch in our souls. Late arrivals huff and puff from the steep climb up the paved trail from the parking lot. The sun is a fully orange sphere, overwhelming the haze and turning the bane of the Smokies – air pollution – into something beautiful. Moments later, the sun has settled, ever so briefly, between slivers of clouds, peering purely through the haze and backlighting the clouds with their silver lining for the day.

As a row of photographers watches, the hushes turn almost to whispers as lovers on the eastern side of the tower find majesty in each other's eyes that distracts them from the western show. The tower empties as the last light turns red and bleeds upward to pinken the unthreatening sky. The sun is but a silhouette, descending into the dark blue, faintly casting gold upward to accent the benign clouds. Appalachians and other Americans, Asians and Indians are here, all drawn by the hope for transcendence in the high country.

Even more leave the tower, intent on making it back to their cars before dark. Sunset has come but light lingers, patiently waiting for the moon to rise. I'm hoping, perhaps wishing, for another memory to be replayed. I was here once when darkness rose in the east and made an orderly march overhead as light retreated in the west, marking the clearest delineation of day and night I'd ever seen or have seen since.

Sanctuary

The temperature has dropped, making it perhaps 10 degrees cooler than when we arrived. I'm glad for our denim shirts. Multiple languages speculate on the landscape that grows darker by the minute. Naked Fraser firs, their green gone, stare starkly, these high-country conifers consumed by a tiny enemy called the balsam wooly adelgid. Looking past the devastation brought by these microscopic murderers of the firs, smiles come easy, and tongues I don't understand exclaim about a scene that needs no explanation. On this concrete structure atop the highest point of the Smokies, memories are made that transcend age and intellect, ethnicity and upbringing.

A slight sliver of moon has risen in the west, just south of where the sun made its last stand. It won't give much light on the way down. We won't need it. We know the way, and the path is clear.

A single star stares from the east, signaling night is coming. All that remain are us and the internationals. We linger and fold our equipment, satisfied with the sunset, content with the end of this day. A last-minute arrival in a sleeveless t-shirt with hair hanging down his back from under his ball cap snaps a shot of the moon and turns his camera on the headlights in line on the Parkway in Pigeon Forge off in the distance. His accent says "Southerner" as his daughter points and shoots as well.

The glory of God's Creation has drawn us here, and, no matter our nationality, our origins, our education, our station, we've seen His majesty painted spectacularly across the western sky. The single star burns brighter as darkness creeps calmly overhead, seemingly borne by the eastern wind that gains strength as night comes closer.

Sanctuary

"When I admire the wonder of a sunset or the beauty of the moon, my soul expands in worship of the Creator."

Gandhi

Baskins Creek
Baskins Cemetery

    Baskins Creek falls softly down below, gently comforting the souls of the Ogles and at least one Floyd buried on the side of this mountain. The stone markers – some square, some with ragged edges, some with tops pointed like church steeples – bear testament to lives lived over 100 years ago, 19th-century lives that could never have imagined their homeland would become a national park. Moss covers their resting place while hardwoods provide shade as evergreens and rhododendron mark the boundary of this sacred place.
    Sunlight filters through the canopy to dapple the graveyard while a hint of wind cools our sweat-soaked backs. The climb from the creek is steep, so steep my first question after catching my breath is, "How

did they get them up here?" The 21 rough-edged stones set in stoic rows on this rugged hillside witness the type of life generations lived before the Park got here.

My son, Reed, wondered aloud about the irony of these settlers' resting places being visited mostly by tourists. What did these folks think when they buried their kin in the side of a mountain? Did they imagine civilization creeping closer? Did they figure their people would be here for generations to come? Or did they simply sing a psalm, say a prayer, bury their dead and go back to work?

Yet, as Reed observed, for all our technological advances, all our modern ways, nothing endures like words carved in a piece of rock. In quiet dignity, through rain and snow and sun, season after season, for a century these stones have stood. Somehow, this place is holy, set apart in time and place, swathed in multiple shades of green, reminding us of the stock we come from while exhorting us to live worthy of our bloodlines and ancestry.

Blue and white above the roof of this secluded chapel on a mountainside call down to us from the world beyond. Yet, we linger – quiet, content and contemplative, at peace and at rest, like the souls resting eternally beside us.

Baskins Creek Falls

It's a short walk from the solitude and solemnity of the cemetery to a riotously refreshing shower in Baskins Creek Falls. Baskins Creek is a benign little branch that feeds through the folds in the foothills of Mt. LeConte and gathers only slightly before sending a small stream over a rock ledge that splatters into a stone trough made by nature to collect the ice-cold water. The trough empties over two outlets perhaps 10 feet up, forming natural showers that some say drew the folks of the Baskins Creek community up the hollow for a Saturday night bath years ago.

Reed took the plunge first, dunking his head under the jarringly frigid water, then gasping before letting out a whoop and a giggle. Stunned by the cold, he went back again. This time he went the whole way under the falls as I struggled out of my boots and shirt, anxious for a dip and determined not to let my son have all the fun.

I whooped and hollered and giggled and shook as the water tumbled over my head. I stepped in and let the falls beat on my neck, laughing and gasping as the tension of another week drained away. Now, the mist wafts coolly across my back as I sit to drip-dry a bit before walking out of the woods. We're alone here, perhaps two miles from town as the crow flies, a mile and a half from the trailhead, as Baskins Creek cascades over the nooks and through the crannies of the rock cliff before gathering again to broaden and form a real creek as it heads down toward the valley.

In this almost-secret place, the traffic jams and tourist rush just down the mountain from us might as well be a million miles away. This trail and these falls are not even listed in many trail books. Some maps omit them as well. All the better for us. Today is a Friday, a low tourist day, giving us silence and serenity, the only noise the rush of the falls and the rustle of the wind in the tree limbs above us. With only a short drive and a short walk, we've left the world of the valley behind and escaped into a world of wonder.

We're taking an unmarked route out of the woods, following Baskins Creek down the mountain, trusting and knowing it will lead us to Gatlinburg. My car waits at the Park boundary on Baskins Creek Road, parked across the street from rental cabins and permanent homes. As we walk down the trail beside the creek, openings appear periodically, giving enough space for the sunlight to flit through, casting ethereal shadows, reminding me of the outskirts of Rivendell, the mythical land of elves from J. R. R. Tolkein's imagination.

Earlier, as we walked the last steps to the falls where the trail runs beside the tiny branch, I watched Reed's face. "Oh, wow!" he said as he realized we had walked to the top of the falls and now looked down on it. The unforgettable and somewhat indescribable joy of discovery lit his face like it did mine the first time I came here. As we walk out, we're walking a path we've never taken before off the mountain, and we worry not about our way. We're blazing a new trail – for us – down the mountain, intent on discovery, content to just be here and be together.

We've laughed and spit and joked and philosophized along the trail, discussing theology and legends, anthropology and archaeology, family and friends and dreams. We've lost ourselves for an afternoon, escaping the present, remembering only the good of the past and not worrying an iota about the future. Though we're just a skip and a jump from the tourist tizzy in downtown Gatlinburg, we've found what we needed – a place to go, to discover, to sense, to savor, to feel and to be.

Sanctuary

"Always in big woods, when you leave familiar ground and step off alone to a new place, there will be, along with feelings of curiosity and excitement, a little nagging of dread. It is the ancient fear of the unknown, and it is your bond with the wilderness you are going into. What you are doing is exploring. You are understanding the first experience, not of the place, but of yourself in that place. It is the experience of our essential loneliness, for nobody can discover the world for anybody else. It is only after we have discovered it for ourselves that it becomes common ground, and a common bond, and we cease to be alone."

Wendell Berry
Writer/Farmer

Walker Sisters Cabin

It's an easy walk to the place where life was anything but easy for the Walker family of Little Greenbrier. John Walker inherited this cabin up in this hollow. His wife's family felled the trees, hewed the logs, stacked the rocks for the fireplace and chinked it all together to keep in the warmth and keep out the weather. When Walker's family grew, he added another cabin to the original and put them both under one roof.

By the standards of the day, a huge corn crib and a sturdy springhouse say that Walker was a prosperous man. Apparently, he was vigorous as well – a rock purportedly discovered on Mt. LeConte, many rugged miles from his home, was carved with his name and recorded that he had killed a bear on LeConte. At least that's what the rock says.

Walker raised a stout-hearted family here in the shadow of Chinquapin Ridge. His daughters – the famed Walker sisters – were a cantankerous crew. When the Park was formed and the landmen came, the Walker sisters wanted nothing to do with them or their money. Even facing the federal government, the sisters wouldn't cede one inch of their homestead, eventually bending Uncle Sam to their will and negotiating, as part of their sales agreement, a lifetime lease on their land that lasted until the last sister died in the 1960s.

The story of the Walker sisters contains the seeds of the sensibilities of the Southern Appalachians. Proud, rugged, resourceful, cantankerous, courageous, distrustful of outsiders – especially the government – the Walker sisters are the spiritual mothers of many of us who call ourselves Appalachians.

Sitting on the steps of the big cabin, I wonder if they refused to move because they were content with their simple life or if they were a bit afraid of the outside world and its blossoming modernity.

Truthfully, they probably felt both. Appalachians, after decades of ridicule and being the butt of at least a few thousand too many jokes, can be a bit defensive and are often unsure of how others view us, how others hear us and our somewhat twangy accent. Given our history of outside actors not necessarily having our best interests at heart, we are still suspicious of those different from us, skeptical of their motives, offended by their arrogance and not at all interested in their desire to "save us." We still pride ourselves on being able to spot a phony a mile away.

But, on this lazy Sunday afternoon, the quietness of this cozy cove is broken only by the bees busily searching for a flower to feed on. Not a leaf stirs on the trees that surround the cabin. This safe, secure place, hidden between ridges, is still, peaceful and comfortable, which leads me to think no one would leave this place voluntarily.

As easy as this summer day is for us, winters had to have had a harder edge for the Walkers. Heating and cooking were done with hand-chopped wood, there was no indoor plumbing, no refrigeration, no electricity even after all those conveniences came to the next valley over. My friend, Joe, and I walked up here a few winters ago. The mud along the creek bank had turned into shards of brown ice that glinted in the morning sun. We could see our breath on each exhale and steam rose from our backs from the sweat we worked up on the walk up the road.

Joe and I noticed the horseshoes used to hang the back window flap on the cabin and marveled at the ingenuity that now looks like a work of art. As we pondered the lives of the pioneers, I aimed a rhetorical question in Joe's general direction. "Who did these people depend on?" I asked. I already knew his answer. "They depended on God," Joe said. "And each other."

Faith, family and community were the foundations of life in the Smokies. These hale and hardy mountain folk loved God and loved their neighbors the best they could, partly out of piety, partly out of necessity. These values still matter to most who call these mountains home. To outsiders, their unaffected egalitarianism, to paraphrase a speech made in the U.S. Senate by former senator and fellow Appalachian from North Georgia Zell Miller, can cause Appalachians to seem simple, unsophisticated, naïve, even ignorant.

Sometimes, frankly, we are. But many of us just don't care about the latest trends, the newest fad, the popular people of popular culture. We've found contentment and meaning in our faith, our families, our communities, and, to be honest, don't really care what the rest of the world has, does or says. That, I think, is what kept the Walker sisters here, what gave them the gumption to fight and befuddle the feds. They had a home. They had family. They were content. They were happy. They had all they needed.

The sun peeks through the high white clouds and blinks through the leaves of the big oak shading the cabin. A quiet breeze rustles the weeds as a plane's growl can barely be heard off in the distance. The bees are still working, but they've yet to find the single purple flower that waves ever so slightly just a few steps outside the back door of the cabin. They go about their work in the quiet comfort of this cove, in no hurry, content to search until they find what they need, at peace with their purpose and place.

No wonder the sisters fought to stay.

Sanctuary

"Heaven is under our feet as well as over our heads."

Henry David Thoreau

Chimney Tops

Memory is a strange thing. I remembered the trail to the Chimneys being steep. It was steeper than I recalled. I remembered the climb up the chimney-like rock formation at the top from years ago. It was higher and harder than I thought.

I had forgotten completely, though, the boulder-strewn stream a few paces from the trailhead. I didn't remember the daisy fields with daubs of yellow and white on a woods-green background, accented with red by Indian paintbrush. I forgot the little boomers – red squirrels – begging and barking on the side of the trail, the tiny cataract falls that peeks from under the rhododendron and the trees with knots on their trunks as big as a bear. I was even surprised to see the Ent-like tree just short of the summit with roots resting on top of the trail – roots so big I half expected Treebeard to groan at Merry and Pippin like he did in the scene in Fanghorn Forest in Tolkein's "Return of the King."

I remembered making it up the trail, to the top of the rocks, without much trouble. Not today. I'm reaping my reward from too much time in a cushioned chair staring at a computer screen, too many years with too few days on the trail. On one of the steep parts down below, I thought, "Maybe I bit off more than I can chew." A ways on, after I caught my breath, I thought, "Maybe I bit off what I need to chew."

I'm a bit astonished now by my first trip up here. Son Reed couldn't have been more than seven or eight years old. We made it to the base of the rock, looked up and started to climb. We moved steadily up the "chimney," hooking our toes on the tiny ledges, grabbing whatever handholds we could find, pulling and pushing up the rock.

Until Reed looked back at the 75- to 85-degree steepness with sharp drops on either side. He froze. I froze and started kicking myself for bringing my kid up a rock steeper than either of us had ever climbed. I said a prayer for help – and asked the Good Lord not to let Reed's mom find out – and told him everything would be okay.

Without thinking, I laid my hand on his back and, surprisingly, he started to climb. He climbed out of my reach and froze again. I caught up and rested my hand on his back. Up he went. We made it to the top of the rock, knees wobbly, psyches somewhat shaken. But I'd seen how a father's hand resting gently on his son's back can give him the courage to climb higher.

A steady stream of muffled vehicle noise climbs up from Highway 441. I can hear the motorcycles gear down as they navigate the loop just up the mountain from the Chimneys parking lot. The sun struggles with some eastern clouds and the faintest of breezes plays up the valley. Mt. LeConte stands hazily to my east. Haze hugs Sugarland Mountain, too, off to the west. The pox of the adelgid is evident on Sugarland, with denuded firs and naked hemlocks, ruined by an adelgid of their own, dotting the mountainside.

A couple of guys from northern Kentucky got to the base of the Chimneys shortly after I arrived. They're heading down Sugarland Mountain to Huskey Gap and were looking for the manway between the Chimneys and Sugarland Mountain Trail. I told them where to find the obscure entry to the manway. Their goal today is a 30-mile loop hike. My goal is four miles, and I'm good with that.

I remembered the manway – an unmaintained and often unmarked path – from a hike from Deep Creek near Bryson City in North Carolina to Gatlinburg years ago. I missed my campsite for reasons I can't remember and ended up pitching my tent on an open spot on the manway. I made no fire and left no trace, but some forest friend stopped by in the night and left a souvenir of scat just outside my tent flap. Barely missed it when I crawled out the next morning.

As I huffed and puffed up the trail this morning, it dawned on me that this is the most I've pushed myself physically for a while. I'm a bit ashamed to admit that, but it's true. We settle into our routines, let the candles on the cake tell us what we can and can't do and slowly get seduced into a sedentary lifestyle.

"Sedentary" is too simple a word, too easy an explanation. It isn't just our bodies that stop moving. Too often, the cumulative circumstances and consequences of life cause our minds and our hearts to slow down and begin to coast. We throw ourselves into our work, numb ourselves with the inanity of "entertainment" – television, the Internet, etc. – and we forget what it's like to dream, to reach, to climb.

Honestly, when I got to the base of the Chimneys this morning, I debated whether to climb the rock. Winded and weary, I paused. Then, just like when Reed was here, I started up. Backpack hugged tight, my camera bag cinched close, up I went, reminding my wobbly self to keep two points of contact with the rock at all times. I worked my way around to a track that looked like it would provide an easy route to the top, or at least a "safer" path, since it hugged the myrtle bushes that somehow grow out of the rock.

Halfway up the rock, I was stuck. My too-short legs couldn't reach the next ledge. I couldn't catch a toehold. I looked at a lateral move to a better track. For a moment, frustration almost gave way to fear. I considered retreat.

Instead, though, I reached higher up the rock and my hand found a finger-width foundation on a little ledge I hadn't seen. With a quick pull, I hoisted myself high enough to throw my leg up to the next toehold. My confidence returned and I scrambled the rest of the way to the top of the rock.

There's no fog rising through the natural hole in the rocks – the "flue" of the chimney – now that the sun has broken free. The crowds are coming. It's time to pick my way down the rocks and head down the mountain. It's warmer now with not much breeze to cool even this high point. I'm satisfied here, sitting on top of this rock, surrounded by the Smokies.

I'm glad I reached a little higher.

Sanctuary

"*The mountains are calling and I must go.*"

John Muir

Grotto Falls

Bears. Our arrival here at this 20-foot falls in this cool cove off Roaring Fork Motor Nature Trail was delayed by bears. A mother bear fed along the road, posing for her portrait, it seemed, since she never missed a chew as the cameras in the car in front of us snapped away, and we did likewise. A bit up the road, a skinny yearling skedaddled across the road, then hightailed it up the side of the mountain.

We'd barely rounded the first bend in the trail to Grotto Falls when hikers on their way out told us about bears up a tree a ways further on. The momma and her two cubs had drawn a crowd with momma foraging up in the highest branches. The cubs seemed too preoccupied with their version of Chutes and Ladders – sliding down one branch, then scampering up another – to really be focused on finding food. We joined the gaggle of hikers and stopped and stared for a while.

Grotto was waiting, still spilling a pair of rivulets around a moss-covered nose of a rock, splashing on striated stones with moss of their own before pooling in front of the cave-shaped overhang that gives the falls its name. The flow was medium but enough to still make a curtain in front of those who wanted to walk behind the falls into the grotto.

I've passed by Grotto more often than I've stopped to stare at it. The falls are about a mile and a half up the Trillium Gap Trail which continues on about five more miles to Mt. LeConte by way of a gap in the mountain where trillium blooms in late spring and early summer. This is the path the llamas take, those spitting pack animals that haul supplies to LeConte Lodge on top of the mountain. The main attraction here is the chance to walk behind a waterfall, stick your hand or head in it and enjoy the constant coolness emanating from the falls.

My knowledge of grottos was extremely limited on my previous trips here. Still is, really. My background as a born-again Baptist turned Charismatic turned Pentecostal before morphing into a lukewarm Lutheran and ending up an Anglican (long story) didn't teach me much about grottos or anything else even vaguely Catholic.

But I can't come to Grotto without thinking about the calm and quiet in the northwestern Kentucky hill country at the Abbey of Gethsemani and the Benedictine brothers there. They took me in for a few days a few years ago, fed me, prayed for me, listened to me, talked a little and loved me when I faced a major crossroads. The tranquility at Gethsemani gave me enough space, enough quiet to hear my heart, hear the whispers of the Holy Spirit and find my way onto the correct path – I hope.

In one way, I'm not so different from Gethsemani's most famous monk and, at least in my circles, everybody's favorite contemplative, Thomas Merton. Like Merton, I want to go the right way, take the right path, but I often wonder if I'm on the right track or have wandered down some dead-end road or into some wild place that exists only in my imagination. Still, to paraphrase an intensely intimate prayer Merton wrote, "I want to please God, but, truthfully, I have no idea if I am pleasing Him. I pray the fact that I want to please Him, pleases Him."

Monastics fascinate me. Set apart from the "real" world, I always thought them odd, wondering about their usefulness in my then utilitarian worldview. How could priests help anyone when they never had contact with anyone except each other? What was the deal with the silence? Why not go start an orphanage or build a school or become a missionary or house the homeless?

Yet, as I observed them at Gethsemani, I saw men who were not just quiet, but men with a quiet spirit. They exhibited none of the frenetic casting about to do good, to do well that characterizes so many religious communities. And, too often, characterizes me. Their ministry was to God, and, through their prayers, the whole world. And to weary, worried, confused, conflicted travelers like me who seek sanctuary, like travelers have for centuries, behind the walls of the monastery.

Several winters ago, I came down off Mt. LeConte on the Bullhead Trail, and the temperature rose as the elevation dropped. My wool cap became too hot so I rolled the ends up a bit to let my ears breathe. Somewhere along the trail, the sun broke through the trees and I saw my shadow – me with my walking stick, my pack and what looked like a friar's cap on my head.

I smiled. The mountains were my monastery, my place to withdraw from the incessant immediacy of the world and quietly talk to God. By then, I knew enough about St. Francis of Assisi – his love of nature, his friendship with wildlife – to see my shadow not as some hare-brained heresy as my somewhat sheltered upbringing would have me believe, but rather as a continuation of centuries of Christian tradition, started by John the Baptist, continued by Christ himself, mimicked by the Desert Fathers, carried forward by Francis and Benedict and the monks at Gethsemani and practiced temporarily by amateurs like me who need time away from the cacophony of civilization.

I embraced the stillness of the wilderness, the languid ways of the woods, the simplicity of walking from one place to the next. I grew to long for time alone with nature and my God, of no use in those moments to anyone, accomplishing nothing other than communing with Him, enjoying His Creation and emptying my soul as I trudged along.

The sun has tucked down below the western ridge and the cool of this cove trends toward cold as air breezes out of the grotto and the spray from the falls dampens the air. The patter and splash of the falls grow hypnotic, soothing the soul, cleansing the spirit, causing me to remember the serenity in the eyes of the monks, aware once again of the healing nature of this place.

Sanctuary

"We need to find God, and he cannot be found in noise and restlessness. God is the friend of silence. See how nature – trees, flowers, grass – grows in silence; see the stars, the moon and the sun, how they move in silence... We need silence to be able to touch souls."

Mother Teresa

The Jump Off

 The fog climbs quickly up the 1000-foot cliff, rattles through the myrtle bushes and dampens my face as I stare out off this lonely ledge hidden on the south side of Mt. LeConte. The wind gusts up from Charlies Bunion, the rock formation down below that draws droves of hikers, but to me lies hidden behind the milky curtain of clouds that rests on the high country today.
 Socked in. What would on a clear day be a beautiful view of the Bunion, the Greenbrier watershed and the Sawteeth off to the east is blanketed by clouds, obscured by fog and mist. This is no lame lovers' leap of a place – the half-mile trek from the Boulevard Trail that leads to Mt. LeConte is rocky and rooty, steep in sections, steep enough to have produced complaints from a hiking group I brought here once. Vegetation clings to the rock face of the precipice, making it look

more benign than most cliffs of desperation. Even on this foggy morn, though, the distance to the valley below is startling, and makes me make sure my feet are firmly planted.

There is a mystery in the mist, a curiosity in the clouds that cover the mountains. The clouds came as I climbed up Mt. Kephart from Newfound Gap. More accurately, I walked up into them as they rested on the mountain. They're so full today that they dampen the limbs and leaves enough to let the wind shake loose a drip here and there, so saturated they sporadically leak a raindrop, full enough to let me know they're here, but benevolent enough not to open up.

One mystery for me about the mist, I guess, is why I feel no disappointment about it blocking the view. My fascination with the fog must come from the quietness it brings, the sense of solitude, the calming effect that comes with the clouds that turn the bushes and rocks on this obscure place into an Impressionistic image.

The trail over Mt. Kephart had a medieval feel as fog wafted through the trees and ferns waved in the wind beside my feet. Moss covered the fallen fir and hemlocks and others hardwoods that could stand no more. Maybe the blanket of clouds feels like a comforter to my soul, giving me a sense of snugness like on a cold winter night in a creaky old house where shadows dance and shapes shift.

Mostly, though, I love the solitude and silence in the London-like fog I encounter in the highlands. I met no one on the trail. There's no one here at the Jump Off. Days like this keep some at home and leave the mountains quieter. I suspect the Bunion will be different, that some will come in hopes the clouds will lift and the day will clear and we'll get a view of the valley.

The Jump Off is the same as it was on January 1, 2000. To mark the new millennium, son Reed and I walked here to watch the sunrise. It was a great idea – see the first sunrise of the new century in the Smokies. We left home at God-thirty, arrived at Newfound Gap before a single Cocke County rooster had crowed and plunged onto the Appalachian Trail in pitch dark.

We had our torches – or flashlights, as we refer to them in the flatlands – and we needed them. There might have been a wink of a star or two when we left the car. The eeriness of hiking in the dark was assuaged by the excitement of adventure, the rush of walking toward the unknown instead of away from it and the knowledge that we would always remember what we did on the first day of the new millennium. But, like today, as we climbed Kephart, we walked up into the mist. We got no help from the moonlight.

Our eyes adjusted, our ears perked as we picked up sounds we wouldn't have heard otherwise. We watched closely for the telltale sign of two little lights staring back at us – a woodland friend – but figured it was too dark and too cold for the black bears to be stirring. Ice covered parts of the trail, but we slipped and slid past those, praying for a miracle clearing of the clouds. It didn't happen. The fog climbed the cliff, the wind ripped across the rocks, and we stamped our feet and kept moving to stay warm as we stared into the white and let the mistiness wash over us.

I had a sense, though, staring into the clouds, of something out there. I knew the sun was rising, knew the eastern ridgeline of the Smokies stretched out before us, knew a new day, a new millennium had come. "Now faith is the substance of things hoped for, the evidence of things not seen," the King James Bible says. Though we could see nothing, our feet were on solid ground, and we knew a new day had dawned – full of substance, we hoped – we just didn't know what it looked like, what it held for us or what the new century would bring.

That unseen sunrise proved prophetic. Life has changed dramatically in ways neither of us could have imagined, and, in many ways, much better than either of us could have hoped for since we were socked in here on that misty New Year's Day.

Reed graduated from high school and is almost finished with college and about to launch a career. I stepped into the 21st century a single parent, a part-time youth pastor, active in several non-profit ministries. Now, I'm ecstatically married, and a second career as a writer has come from somewhere. We could see none of that through the fog of the future on January 1, 2000.

So, here I am again, in the quiet, cloistered solitude of the Jump Off, blanketed by clouds, fascinated by the fog, caressed by the mist, as uncertain as ever, yet confident that, if I keep walking, the sun will shine again.

Charlies Bunion

Well. That was quick. I'm on top of Charlies Bunion – the very top – basking in the sunshine, listening to the winds swish and sway as they serenade me with their soothing symphony. Gone is my denim shirt. I've put away the thought of breaking out the gloves I started to unpack at the Jump Off.

In less than an hour's time since I left the Jump Off, only a few hundred feet drop in elevation, about two miles by trail and not too many steps along the path, the world is completely different. Gone are the fog and clouds and mist. The temperature is 20 degrees warmer. I can see clearly. The Sawteeth stagger off to the east. The Smokies roll north into Sevier County and south toward the home of an early Park enthusiast named Charlie who, legend has it, climbed up here to this rock outcropping, bunions on his feet be damned.

LeConte is picture perfect to the west, and the Jump Off has kicked off its bedclothes to bask in the climbing sun.

They say to expect the unexpected in the Smokies, but I surely didn't expect this. Idyllic is the word that comes to mind. Gentle breeze. Just-right sun. The wind quietly comforts as it rustles and rushes up from the valley as I sit alone on top of the rock, looking out at the world for miles around. The walk and the fog and the clouds and the cold were worth it.

A guy in running shoes and citified running gear showed up while I took my lunch on the main rock below. I asked where he was headed, and he said he was just doing some trail-running. I asked how he was handling the rocks on the trail, and he said he grew up in Seattle and the rocks were bigger there. He bragged about Mt. Rainier. I bragged about Mt. LeConte and Clingmans Dome and told him these are the highest mountains in the Appalachians. He took a photo with one of those one-time use cameras, asked some directions and took off. He was nice except when he bragged about how tall those Washington mountains are. Westerners are like that – they brag about their mountains. Whatever.

Seeing him out for some exercise reminded me of my own gonzo adventure years ago. When I went into the wild just to prove I could do it, I breezed by the Bunion and barely blinked at its beauty, too.

A friend of mine had told me about a manway from down at Porters Creek up to the Appalachian Trail. It wasn't listed on any maps. References to it in guidebooks were few. But my friend told me where to start, so I took off, hiked to the end of Porters Creek Trail, fortified with food and forded the creek. I was fully equipped – signal mirror in case I got hurt, air horn to honk at search parties if I got lost, an emergency blanket, matches, maps, compass, etc. Then, as soon as I crossed Porters Creek, I walked up on the biggest pile of bear scat I'd ever seen.

Flummoxed by fate, I reached for the best defense mechanism I could find. The hills came alive to the sound of my air horn. Long, loud blasts shrieked through the back country. I didn't see any bears.

The first part of the manway was easy to follow, picking its path along Porters Creek and its tiny tributaries. As the mountain turned steeper, the path became less decipherable, crossing the creek, appearing here, reappearing over there, until finally, it was gone. I knew if I kept going up I would make it to the AT. I also knew if I drifted too far west, I would be trapped at the bottom of the Bunion, hemmed in by the sheer rock cliffs that surround it.

I had splashed up the creek for just a few minutes when I saw my salvation – a cairn. Those rocks, stacked in the shape of a pyramid, lifted my spirits and let me know someone had come this way before. And, they cared enough about those who came after them to mark the way. That cairn might as well have been the marker Moses put down after he and God led the Israelites out of Egypt. It marked my deliverance from confusion.

Either the cairns gave out, or I took a wrong turn near the top, but the end of the manway called for hand-over-hand climbing. My spirit soared as I sensed the summit. Pulling myself up by roots, a strange sound came between my gasps for air. Talking. Singing, maybe. The trail was nearby. I hurried harder, unsure of where I would land on the AT and hoping to ask the unseen hiker if he had passed the Bunion, since I would know my way from there.

I popped up onto the trail out of nowhere, flushed with endorphins, giddy that I'd done it. "Hey!" I yelled. "Where's the Bunion?" The unsuspecting hiker jumped to a stop, whirled on his heel and turned white as a ghost. "Did you pass the Bunion already?" I asked again. "I, uh, uh, I, uh, uh, I don't know," he said. "Okay, thanks," I said and headed east on the AT, deciding it didn't matter if

I saw the Bunion that day or not. Only later would I realize how shocking a nasty, naturally high man popping up on the side of the trail must have seemed to a guy just out for a walk in the woods, five miles from the trailhead.

The day has turned glorious, the threat of rain completely gone, the only clouds like puffy pillows held aloft by lullaby winds. I could nap here. I hear voices down below, signaling an end to my idyll. I can see Douglas Lake off in the distance, marking the place of my mother's people, their homesites under water now. My paternal grandmother's people came from Greenbrier, just down the mountain from where I stand.

Muir was right; coming to the mountains is like coming home.

Sanctuary

"It is not the mountain we conquer but ourselves."

Sir Edmund Hillary

Gregory Bald

The trip to this acres-big bald with views of Cades Cove to the north and toward Fontana Lake to the south exposed the essential elements of a Great Smoky Mountains' backcountry experience, ranging from the bucolic to the invigorating, from the rugged to the exhilarating.

Cades Cove was covered with mist as I drove through not long after sunrise. A dozen or more wild turkeys wandered in the field just past the Cove's entrance gate, strutting and stretching to greet the new day. One strong fellow flew, confidently, majestically, so strongly he had to taxi a bit when he touched down, running a few yards after his powerful landing.

Further on in the Cove, a young doe walked up into the woods while further on still a 10-point buck with velvety antlers grazed beside another beautiful doe. Cades Cove, like it is most days, was tranquil, welcoming, soothing as it awakened to the Labor Day weekend.

Parsons Branch Road revealed the ruggedness of the mountains before my feet ever touched the trail. A narrow, one-lane, one-way, eight-mile stretch of wilderness road that connects Cades Cove to U.S. 129 – aka The Dragon for its several and serpentine curves – in North Carolina, Parsons Branch is steep and occasionally rutted with some minor stream fordings thrown in for good measure. It's so isolated and little traveled that a gray squirrel defied my SUV and scooted along up the middle of the road for hundreds of feet to let me know this was his wood, and he wasn't going to cede his territory easily to my mechanical invader.

Quiet engulfed me when I stepped from the borrowed SUV, the only sounds the bing of the engine cooling and the muffled rush of jet engines from the airplanes already at altitude after taking off from McGhee Tyson Airport many miles in the distance in Blount County. Back down the trail, a silent wind tickled the leaves, causing them to wiggle and wave like woodland mimes.

Not far from the trailhead, a crash echoed through the little cove the trail was winding through. My heart fluttered and my adrenaline spiked as I looked up the mountain to see the backside of a big black bear hurrying up the hillside through the undergrowth above me, heading higher toward the top of the mountain, the same direction I was going.

In an instant, my mind rushed to an outfitter's shop in Montana where a clerk told us not to bother buying whistles to scare off the grizzlies. "They hear the whistle," he said, "and say, 'Oh, goody! Dinnertime!'" He told us to sing or talk while we walked to alert the grizzlies we were in the area, and they would simply avoid us. "Most of the time," he said with a smile.

So, in the next instant, I sang. And picked up a stick. For whatever reason, an old hymn popped out of my mouth: "I heard an old, old story, how a Savior came from glory..." If I remember correctly, it's the same song I belted out when I walked up on a bear on the Rainbow Falls Trail on my way up Mt. LeConte several years ago. Strange. "Victory in Jesus" must be my bear song. But it worked. My singing must have scared him deeper into the woods. Half an hour on, I ditched the stick and let the woodlands' ears rest. I thought I heard a sigh.

It's beautiful here on the bald. The wild azaleas flamed out a couple of months ago, dropping their reds and oranges until next summer. The wind is stronger on top but refreshing. The noonday sun paints my neck as I look out through a low haze at Cades Cove and the western end of the Smokies. Turns out I needed today.

Sanctuary

We admitted my dad to the hospital last night. He had fallen and hurt his leg and hadn't eaten much for a couple of days. Tests revealed his blood sugar was dangerously elevated and his kidney function was severely diminished. The day before, I learned my cousin's son was dead of a gunshot wound. The family gathered to comfort his grandparents – my aunt and uncle – in their sudden, tragic loss. He was only 14. Tonight I go to the funeral home.

And I came to the woods anyway. I wasn't sure I should, but my wife and my mother shooed me on. "There's nothing you can do right now," they said. So here I lay in the grass on top of the mountain, brushing away flies, sipping on my water bottle, letting the wind comfort me, praying for my family and practicing my temporary monasticism.

The solitude and silence are almost alarming in this isolated section of the Smokies. There is space here – space for reflection, space for refreshing, space for healing, space for prayer. While others attend to the pastoral duties and temporal needs like holding hands, hugging necks, wiping brows, I sit alone on a mountain and, like the monks at Gethsemani, ask God to transcend time and space to heal my dad, comfort my relatives and work in the world. It is a strange way, but a good way. I pray it's the right way.

With the wind whipping across the extinguished flame azaleas and the sun warming perfectly out of an almost cloudless sky, I'm tempted to pitch a permanent tent here, like St. Peter proposed on the Mount of Transfiguration where Christ and two other men of mountains, Moses and Elijah, radiated God's glory. As perfect as this place is today, this bald I share a name with, like my monasticism it is meant to be a way station rather than a destination. My life and my place are back down below with my family, my people, engaged with them to try, in some small way, to make their world a bit better.

Oh, there are plenty of glorious vistas in the valley – the faces of a family loving each other through a hard time, the love that endures the hardships and heartaches that come from being kin. Even in the simple things like taking a meal together, listening to the troubles and triumphs of our fellow human beings – these are glorious things to view if we can but see them.

This transcendent field of grasses and azaleas and wild blueberries, the panoramic views into Cades Cove and east across the expanse of the Smokies, the whisper of the wind and the warming of the sun herald a hint of heaven. But the glory of my mountaintop monastery cannot be captured, cannot be replicated in the lower, everyday world. I can only pray that I store some of it in my soul, hide a part of it in my heart so others can see it in my face, hear it in my voice and feel it in my touch.

Glory such as this should be shared.

Sanctuary

"If I can put one touch of rosy sunset into the life of any man or woman, I shall feel that I have worked with God."

G.K. Chesterton

Sugarlands Quiet Walkway

The roar of the West Prong of the Little Pigeon River drowns the sounds of civilization that reverberate on the roadway less than half a mile from here. Perched on a rock while my wife, Diane, dangles her feet in the frosty river, my mind is now miles away from the troubles of town. A fly fisherman picks his way upstream, hiding behind boulders before carefully casting his lure into the semi-still pools that gather the waters only briefly before they crash on down the mountain.

This is a perfect place for a Sunday afternoon. These woods are still warm – we've not gained enough elevation on this summer day to feel much temperature difference from the lowlands – but the river throws off a hint of coolness as it tumbles past. Butterflies danced along the trail, settling sometimes on the flowers beside this short, quiet path, their underside perfectly speckled orange to camouflage them as they lit on flowers colored the same. The woods are splotched with greens and grays while the river welcomes travelers to wet a hook or their toes.

It's been years since I've been here. And, through the tick of time, most of my visits run together. I've made quick getaways to this walkway, most often to let the roar of the river clear the clamor in my head. On another summer visit, I came prepared, stripped to my swimsuit, ventured into the pool just over there, ducked under the water and let the river run over me, washing away my worries.

I spent Christmas Day here one year, wandering through the paths along the river, trying to will my mind well. My kids were young, their mom and I were divorced and it was her turn for Santa to visit the kids at her house. We had a fine Christmas Eve, complete with gifts and gaiety at my parents' house, keeping a tradition that will one day be no more. We opened gifts at my house, snapped photos, maybe even read the story of Christ's birth from St. Luke. Then, the children went away.

Christmas dawned cold and empty, like my house and my heart. I came to the Smokies, to Sugarlands, picking a short drive and a short walk so I could get back for lunch with my parents. Snow lingered along the walkway and covered the higher elevations. As I made my way down the graveled grade, a flock of turkeys started from my steps and their sudden flight sent my heart flapping. Ice covered the corners of the stream and made rock-hopping too treacherous for me on that day. I walked in the woods, cried and prayed. Cold never felt so comforting.

On another winter day, I cut across to this quiet walkway from the Huskey Gap Trail. I'd started in Bryson City, North Carolina, hiked up Deep Creek, crossed Mt. Collins in the snow and descended the Sugarland Mountain Trail to Huskey Gap. My goal was Gatlinburg and I followed the footpaths north from where I sit right now until they ended not far from the Sugarlands Visitor Center. I could walk down the road to pick up the Gatlinburg Trail or shinny across a huge, snow-covered log, bushwhack to the Old Sugarlands Trail and take it to the trail that would take me to town. I chose the less traveled way.

Worried about my footing, I put my pack in front of me and pushed it along as I scooted across the log on my backside. I cut through the woods, picking up game paths occasionally, but sometimes pushing through the undergrowth until I found the trail. By the time I got to Gatlinburg, the sun was out, the weather warm and snow long gone.

The water rushing over the rocks, cutting its way down the mountainside and imperceptibly wearing at the boulders is pristine, mostly untouched by humans, leaving it virtually free of pollution. I tested these waters one summer about three decades ago as part of an undergraduate independent research course. I examined the levels of fecal contamination just down the river from here, took another sample below Gatlinburg, one slightly north of Pigeon Forge and a fourth in Sevierville just before the West Prong joins the Middle Prong of the Little Pigeon.

Not surprisingly, the water here was clean of human excrement, showing only traces of contaminants which likely came from groundwater runoff. The Gatlinburg site was by far the most polluted while water collected near Pigeon Forge had grown significantly cleaner and, by the time the river reached Sevierville, most of the effects of Gatlinburg's egregious release of contaminants had disappeared. Still, the river has been posted with danger signs below Gatlinburg for years now, showing the irony of a place being loved to death.

The crashing, whirling run of the river over rocks and around bends had renewed it, rejuvenated it, revived it by the time it had tumbled the many miles from the mountains to the flatter lands near Sevierville. Contaminants had been removed and oxygen had been replenished, allowing aquatic flora and fauna to return to the river. The river came back to life simply by continuing to flow, continuing to tumble in what, to the casual observer on the riverbank, seems a haphazard dash down from the mountains.

A family has come to sit by the stream and snap photos a ways downstream from where Diane still dangles her feet. I didn't come prepared today to beat the heat with an icy plunge. But, the sun has edged off me now, and I can feel the draft of the river. The fly fishermen have worked on upstream, leaving us to listen to the rush of the river as we let the mountain sounds soothe our souls.

These rambunctious, relentless waters will make their way to the valley, to Knoxville and beyond, where they will turn turbines to create electricity, float barges to facilitate commerce and carry watercraft holding folks at play. Eventually, these very waters will join the Mississippi and empty into the Gulf of Mexico where they'll climb back into clouds and perhaps someday dump their droplets into the highlands again.

But, today, on an easy Sunday afternoon, the wild yet welcoming waters cool our feet, cover the sounds of civilization and rush on past, even as we have paused beside them.

Sanctuary

"The best remedy for those who are afraid, lonely or unhappy is to go outside, somewhere where they can be quiet, alone with the heavens, nature and God. Because only then does one feel that all is as it should be and that God wishes to see people happy, amidst the simple beauty of nature."

Anne Frank

Little Greenbrier Schoolhouse

There are tombstones in the schoolyard. Thirty-nine markers for 59 lives – 20 graves in the cemetery are unmarked – lives lived in this cove before the national park, before electricity, before it took a bond issue or a tax increase to build a school. The oldest marked grave dates to 1891, though some of the unmarked plots surely came earlier. The harshness of mountain life is evidenced by the number of infants interred.

The settlers here in Little Greenbrier cut the trees, split the logs and built the desks, all without a federal earmark or an infusion of cash from any form of government. Built in 1881, the school grew to house 75 children by 1924. A 1909 photo on the Park display outside the schoolhouse shows 19 kids ranging in age from six or so to late teens. The school operated until 1935, lasting a year or so after the Park was formed.

The graveyard outside, of course, wasn't sponsored by the school. A Primitive Baptist church used this building, too. In fact, though historical records are sparse, my suspicion is the church came first, then the school, following a pattern that continues to this day in developing countries. People of faith were and are people of the Book and, after meeting their basic needs, became people of books who saw education as the avenue toward a more prosperous life.

We've seen the same thing happen in Kenya. In the mid-1990s, a group from here in the Appalachian foothills went to Nairobi to help start churches. I was on a team that went into Kayole, a suburb of Nairobi, which was home to a rock quarry. The Asian company that owned the quarry provided its workers with housing, a paycheck and not much else. Water came from a community faucet. The facilities were incredibly unclean outhouses. Trash heaped at the end of the rows of concrete-block homes. The poverty was paralyzing. The only connection to modernity came from a black-and-white television hung from the ceiling in a tiny one-room, concrete-block community building. We came. We preached. We left.

One of our team – Cyndy Waters – couldn't get the Kenyans out of her head. Or heart. After much prayer and discussion, she returned the next year to the area where we had worked. The nascent church had died. The people told her they appreciated her efforts, but what they really needed was a school. With hardly any support, she got permission to use the community building, set about finding a teacher and a preacher and started a church and a school in that dank, dark building. Money was tight, times were hard and there were more than a few fits and starts. But, the people prayed, she persevered, and the community came together.

Now, over a decade later, the school has grown out of that one-room building, expanding to twelve grades and many more classrooms. The church grew, too, and a new building was recently dedicated. The secondary school graduated its first class last year. Faith started the work. Hope kept the project going through difficult times. And, love of God and love of neighbors kept the Americans giving and the Kenyans working. Today, a community has been and continues to be transformed by an effort that started in a church that also housed a school.

As the late afternoon sun streams through the window, the back of the seat in front of me doubles as my desktop. It's dead silent here in this hollow, not a leaf moving outside, the day done for tourists, leaving the lonely woods to a writer and his thoughts.

I cannot come to this cove without thinking about the intersection of faith and learning. For all the talk of anti-intellectualism in the Southern Appalachians, places like this challenge that assumption. The people of the mountains absolutely trusted in God, prayed and praised in their backwoods' way and were bound together by common struggles, common trials and an uncommon faith. The hardscrabble life held its own rewards, but the mountain folk still needed to hold onto hope of a heavenly reward.

The bonds of kin and community were strong, the mountains too rugged to be faced alone. These folks hidden here in this hollow – 500 miles from Washington, D.C., 250 miles from Nashville, 25 miles from the nearest county seat – came together to build a school to better their children. The Southern Appalachians are still populated by people who simply put their collective shoulder to a problem and push together to solve it without waiting for a bureaucrat to bless them.

This place symbolizes the soul of the Smokies. In this rugged, isolated place, pioneering people came to carve a life out of the sides of the mountains. Here they lived a life of faith that sustained them, their families, their communities. The church served them spiritual sustenance while at the same time being a gathering place where life and death were shared.

Vigorous churches – large and small – still live in the foothills of the Smokies, oftentimes oblivious to the fast-fading fads foisted on America by the culture vultures in New York and Los Angeles, still vibrantly functioning as the place where community is formed, where brothers and sisters in the faith become family, where joys are celebrated and tragedy is shared.

The spiritual descendants of the mountain people of Little Greenbrier, no matter where they live in America, still see the church as the primary vehicle for personal growth and societal change. Like their ancestors did here in this quiet cove, millions of Americans turn to the church for comfort and community and, from their shared convictions, seek to solve the ills of society by prayer and action.

Yes, there are tombstones in the schoolyard. But, the spirit that brought change to this tiny Appalachian outpost, the spirit that sought better for the next generation, is alive and well. From this hidden hollow to the grand cities of Europe, from log churches in the backwoods to soaring cathedrals on the plains, from the Southern Appalachians to the suburbs near the Serengeti, from steeple to steeple across the earth, the church lives. And the Spirit that shook the world at Pentecost still transforms lives and changes the world, one heart, one family, one community at a time.

Sanctuary

"*Come forth into the light of things, let nature be your teacher.*"

William Wordsworth

Ramsey Cascades

It took an hour and a half for the trail to wipe the sleep from my eyes and brush the cobwebs from my brain. My body was willing, but my spirit was too weak to dash into the dark and tackle the strenuous trail that leads up to the always-cool Cascades. So, I flopped in bed, turned off the alarm, dallied a bit in the bath before chunking my staples – peanut butter and honey on wheat, sunflower kernels, an apple and four bottles of water – into my pack and lighting out for Greenbrier.

Maybe the steepness of the trail, especially the last infuriating half-mile, dampened my enthusiasm. The path basically follows Ramsey Prong straight up the mountain with few switchbacks or flat spots to let a guy catch his breath. The first mile and a half is an old jeep road that gave access to a now-defunct fire tower that used to stand on Greenbrier Pinnacle. Though steep in parts, the easy walking on a roadbed most always lulls this hiker into a gait unfit for the last two and a half miles.

Past the looped turnaround on the jeep road, Ramsey gets serious, relentlessly uphill over roots and rocks, and the difficulty of the hike can distract from the beauty. Long rhododendron tunnels are unseen as eyes are trained on the trail to avoid tripping on roots. Massive boulders, some covered with moss that makes them seem more benign, might be missed as the hiker huffs up the trail. Fields of ferns can be forgotten when walking on the few flat places that let the heartbeat decline and respiration decrease. One could walk right past the giant tulip poplars – two stand like silent sentries beside the trail and, nearby, the granddaddy rises, more than three arm-spans of a man around – if not for the need to sometimes stop and breathe.

But the last several steps madden me. The trail turns north away from the river perhaps a mile from the Cascades. It makes for easier walking with the elevation gains made gentler by fewer rocks and a switchback or two. As the trail turns back to the river, though, the steepness returns. No matter how many times I come here, when I again hear the roar of the river, my mind can't help but think, "I'm there." Except I'm not. The trail slogs on.

The tops of the trees started catching the sunrise early on the trail this morning, but the light didn't hit my mind until much later. Maybe it was the three newspaper columns, one speech and five difficult days at my day job. Perhaps my musty mind was but the aftermath of my dad's hospitalization, two deaths in the family and a break-in at my daughter's apartment with too little time to process the stress. Could be birthday 51 yesterday served as a subtle subtext to muffle my mind.

Regardless, an hour and a half in this morning, after huffing and puffing and sweating for a while, I rounded a turn, crossed a bridge, climbed up the trail a bit and saw a ray of sunshine coming through the canopy to spotlight a moss-covered rock. In an instant, the fog burned away, the mist dissipated, the cobwebs cleared and clarity came. The small beam from above warmed my soul.

So, on I tramped on my 51-year-old legs, stopping when I needed, pausing when I wanted, not caring (much) how long it took me to reach the falls. I'm not good with the mundane, the monotonous, and, truth be told, I know no one who really enjoys the drudgery of trudging uphill. Sure, we enjoy reaching the summit, seeing the views, completing the climb – oftentimes to be able to brag, to ourselves if not to others, about how high we've gone, how far we've walked – but there's just not much joy in an uphill journey. Again, though, I learned the value of getting up, getting going, taking the first step and continuing to put one foot in front of the other until the way lightens, and I reach my next way station.

Would to God – literally! – I could remember that always. To always remember that light comes after darkness, the path eventually flattens, beauty will surprise along the way would make life, as an aphorism I once hung on my office wall said, "not a problem to be solved, but a mystery to be lived."

Instead, frankly, I too often live a sort of daily deism, confident that God is real, that He cares about me, that I have a relationship with him, that He has, as I understand it, given me the tasks that I undertake day by day, but He isn't to be troubled with the details. This is the deism of, for one, Thomas Jefferson, who acknowledged God yet saw His role as winding up the world and letting it go, with us poor, pitiful – and pitiable – humans left to our own devices, able to go no further than our human strength.

Yet that flies in the face of all I've ever known, ever believed, even ever experienced. "Surely God has bigger things to worry about than whether my bills get paid," is an example of the answer often offered when the question is whether God cares about the details of daily life. But, if God is our heavenly Father, surely He is more capable than I am. When I make sure my son, for instance, has enough money to pay his tuition and still buy food while at the same time advising him about career choices and discussing the state of the nation or the world, am I not equally able to provide guidance on the small things and the big picture? Undoubtedly, we've made God over into our image, much smaller than He is, less powerful, in our eyes, than the Creator of the universe He surely is. We are wrong.

 The Cascades are flowing fine, even without much rain lately, and this little cove is as cool as always. The sun has steadily moved westward and the light has changed. Though the sun was nowhere near the Cascades when I arrived, the trees just downstream from the falls that miraculously cling to a rock as big as a Winnebago now collect the light they need while the water dances from rock to rock to rock as it tumbles from the top of the falls before rushing past me and washing away the last of the must from my mind.

Sanctuary

"Hiking a ridge, a meadow, a river bottom, is as healthy a form of exercise as one can get."

William O. Douglas
Supreme Court Justice

Rocky Top

Somewhere in Knoxville, Tennessee, on this September day, the Pride of the Southland Marching Band's trumpeters and trombonists are preparing for game time. Somewhere in Big Orange Country, surely at least one somebody among the legions of Volunteer fans is loosening up his or her vocal chords as the University of Tennessee prepares to play the University of Florida in football this afternoon. And, surely by now, someone, somewhere is already singing the chorus of UT's bluegrassy theme song "Rocky Top."

Meanwhile, I'm sitting on it. Rocky Top, I mean. The real one. The one you have to hike six miles to get to. This small, jagged field of rocks ringed by myrtle and rhododendron sits in the clouds today, the view of Fontana Lake and Cades Cove occluded by mist for now. The clouds shift just enough, though, to give a glimpse into the valley below. A mostly clear day down below means nothing here in the mountains.

It took longer to get here than I remembered. The mile or so from Spence Field along the Appalachian Trail was brutal, leaving me sucking wind and rubber-legged. It's been a decade and a half or more since I came to this high-country hideaway. Not many people know about the real Rocky Top. Even fewer come here. They just know the song.

Actually, Rocky Top sits on the backcountry equivalent of the Appalachian autobahn. The Appalachian Trail crosses Rocky Top, and I've never been here that folks didn't buzz by on their way to the next shelter, putting in the next leg of their journey on America's most famous hiking highway. Two guys passed by already and asked me to snap a photo as they hustled on toward Mollies Ridge Shelter via Spence Field. They told me two of their buddies were behind them, sucking wind like I did, struggling up Thunderhead Mountain.

I was here years ago sunning myself, feeling cocky about my accomplishment of hiking up from Cades Cove, basking in my imagined glory when, off in the distance, I heard voices coming from Thunderhead to the east and looked and saw a couple of tiny dots moving my direction. I continued to bronze and returned to my reverie about my powerful hiking prowess.

The dots turned into people as they came closer, and when they stepped onto Rocky Top, I was somewhat surprised to see a woman in her 50s and her mother. Yes, her mother. "Where'd you come from?" I asked, using proper backcountry etiquette and an appropriate high-country conversation starter. They mentioned a shelter, and I followed up: "Where ya headed?"

"Fontana," the younger one told me. My prowess was now looking puny. "Yes, after we finish this leg, Mother will have hiked the entire Appalachian Trail," the daughter said. My pride fell and my ego deflated. The mom had hiked the AT in sections, wearing out her offspring and several pairs of boots, and was approaching the end of her 2,100-plus mile adventure. I kept my 6-mile walk to myself.

I pushed myself this morning. The 6-plus miles uphill to here is the most I've done since I started this project. My legs felt crampy, my rest stops grew frequent and, as bad as I hate to admit it, I thought about stopping short. I suppose there would have been no shame in that. There's no scoreboard in the backcountry, no seasonal standings, no playoff, no Super Bowl. Except in my mind.

In there, hidden from all to see but me, I can't help but set goals and seek to climb higher. Everest is not on my agenda, and I've learned, to a degree, to be content in the valley. But, once my feet touch the trail, I monitor my time and distance, partly out of practicality, but partly because I want to know how far I've gone and how fast I've gone to see if I can make my schedule. Woe is me!

Sometimes, I wish I could just walk and enjoy the scenery, far and fast and schedule be damned.

I'm doing better at stopping and staring. I have to. My body is slowly pushing itself into high-country condition, but it's not there yet. So, I stop more than I used to, notice things I would never have seen, enjoy the cool and the quiet and the views because I'm forced to go slower. It's a good thing, really.

St. Paul wrote about contentment and said he had learned to live joyfully whether in poverty or in plenty, whether, as the King James Version of the Bible puts it, "abase" or "abound." As a young man, he had been a rising star in the Hebrew establishment until he encountered Christ on the road to Damascus. Ostracized immediately by his old colleagues, not initially accepted or trusted by his new community, he eventually was shipwrecked, beaten and imprisoned, even as he was elevated as an apostle.

Somehow, Paul learned when to push and when to be patient, when to rest and when to work, when to leave and when to stay, and to be content no matter what. My prayer this morning asked for that kind of wisdom, that kind of contentment; "When do I climb and when do I sit? When do I go to the high country and when do I rejoice at my place in the valley? Help me," I prayed, "to know when to push, when to be patient, when to rush, when to rest and help me to remember that You are with me wherever I am, whatever I'm doing. That, after all, is the most joyous of thoughts."

The mist has cleared, the wind has turned cool while the sun remains hot, reddening my cheeks and forehead. I've rested, eaten, hydrated and written, even taking time to lie back on the real Rocky Top and take a catnap, the 100,000 folks gathering for the football game in Knoxville the furthest thing from my mind. Thunderhead is visible now a half mile to the east. I think I hear the mountain calling me.

Sanctuary

"*The trail is the thing, not the end of the trail. Travel too fast and you miss all you are traveling for.*"

Louis L'Amour

Thunderhead Mountain

The clouds are so close I can touch them, literally, at least the ethereal ones that occasionally rush across the valley, bump into the mountain, rise up the ridge and climb quickly over the rhododendron thicket atop Thunderhead. For those who've climbed it, it's just "Thunderhead." No need to say "Mountain." Such is its rugged reputation.

Today, though, the summit of this ominously named mountain is benign. Unthreatening clouds hold no hint of rain, the only notice of the weather the hot sun beating on my neck followed by a too-cool breeze that alerts me that autumn is upon us.

The joy to be found on Thunderhead is not the view from the summit. The rhododendron thicket on top is dense, impenetrable even, and, if some kind soul hadn't built a rock platform that lets hikers peep over the thicket to see some mountains to the south, there would be no view at all. No, the joy of Thunderhead's summit is that you're on it. It is a mountain to be climbed just for climbing's sake, just so you can say you've summited it.

There are surely steeper climbs in the world, perhaps a few even in the Smokies, but Thunderhead is sadistic. On an approach from the east on the Appalachian Trail, Thunderhead looms all day in the mind, almost mocking, daring you to do it. Then, before the mountain ever starts, another knob rises from nowhere to drain legs and lungs before the hiker hits the hell of Thunderhead.

Coming up the mountain from the west, the brutality begins at Spence Field, and what looks like an easy walk to Rocky Top and then along the AT up to Thunderhead sets the heart thumping and the thighs groaning. There's little rational reason to go through the agony to simply stand in a thicket and look at a sign that says,

"Thunderhead Mtn. Elev. 5,527'." Sure, there's a glimpse of the landscape in North Carolina from on top of the rocks stacked near the sign, but there are many other views in many places easier to reach.

Ah, but the joy from having made the climb. Sublime. Supreme. A wee bit intoxicating. At least to the point of tipsy. For there's something about going hard to get high that just lifts one's chin and puffs one's chest. I've noticed my posture is straighter, my shoulders back a bit, problems less peeving and satisfaction more prevalent after a hard hike to the high country. It's no wonder us backcountry afficionados can quickly turn into backcountry braggarts.

"See the football game yesterday?" somebody might ask tomorrow at church. "No, I hiked up to Rocky Top then on to Thunderhead," Usually, kind questioners will simply say, "Oh." Less kind will roll their eyes. In the thin air, our self-satisfaction can quickly expand into smugness, and we bring it back down the mountain with us. For my people – the high, hard hikers – and for me, I apologize.

Son Reed and I hiked up to the southern foot of Thunderhead several summers ago. A writer since he could hold a crayon, Reed saw the name "Bone Valley" on one of my maps. Bone Valley intrigued him. He was maybe 13.

The name actually comes from the story of a farmer who was driving his cattle either up or down the mountain to graze them on Thunderhead before the Park was formed. The poor man was surprised by either a too-early or too-late in the season snowstorm that trapped the cattle. They all died, and the valley was littered with their bones.

Reed, though, imagined Bone Valley held a secret government installation that had to do with dinosaurs or atomic weapons, I can't remember which. So we took a boat across Fontana Lake from the marina, hiked up Hazel Creek, camped and, the next day, made over half a dozen stream crossings hiking up to Bone Valley.

Sanctuary

We didn't see any signs of secret goings-on, but we found the foundation of a hunting lodge built by the founder of the Kress Department Stores. We saw the Creed Hall cabin, the most remote Park-maintained structure in the Great Smoky Mountains National Park. We saw the remnants of the logging town of Proctor where some of the buildings still stand, and historical displays tell the town's story. And, to our surprise, we found a wetlands area – a bizarrely different ecosystem than any I've seen in the Smokies – apparently the result of strategically constructed beaver dams.

We were in the area of the Smokies famed mountaineer and writer Horace Kephart called "the back of beyond." Kephart tramped these mountains, met the people, told their stories and was a vigorous advocate for preserving the scenic beauty and the history of the people. At the head of Bone Valley, we looked up at Thunderhead looming over us, safe in its shadow, content that we'd walked into the backcountry. Our adventure ended with an idyllic boat ride across a totally placid Fontana Lake with local legend Lester at the helm.

Now, I sit on top of the back of beyond, glad I pushed higher this time, glad I kept walking, glad the sun is shining on top of Thunderhead. And, to think, I almost stopped short. I almost stayed on Rocky Top because I was tired, unsure of whether to go on, not convinced the walk the rest of the way to Thunderhead would be worth it.

As it turns out – which I had forgotten – most of the hard hiking was behind me by the time I made it to Rocky Top. Thunderhead is only half a mile from Rocky Top and the trail is down then up, but the AT took me through mountain meadows alive with high country vistas and glorious views down to North Carolina. Rocks along the way had the distinctive white blaze – a six-inch by two-inch strip of white paint – of the AT painted on them while ferns and flowers lined parts of the trail.

I wonder how many times I've stopped short in life, only steps from my destination, only a few minutes from making it where I intended to go. I wonder how many fantastic views I've missed because I was tired or talked myself out of going on, going the extra mile, the extra half-mile, that could have made all the difference.

Thunderhead is under my feet. The scenery has given me a second wind. The summit has emboldened me. What? What's that, you ask? Well, yes, yes I did. I just climbed Thunderhead.

Sanctuary

"Today is your day!
Your mountain is waiting.
So... get on your way."

Theodor S. Geisel
(Dr. Seuss)
From "Oh, the Places You'll Go!"

Spence Field

Spence Field is no longer the expansive grassy field it was the last time I came here more than a decade ago. Left alone to return to its natural state, succession proceeds apace, with some sections of Spence covered with briers, others sprouting colorful weeds with flowers abloom that are covered with bees and butterflies, while trees stand taller and block the views off to the south.

But, the Spence Field Hilton, aka the Spence Field Shelter, is posh compared to what it used to be. This heavily used shelter along the Appalachian Trail has been expanded since I was here last. A high-roofed porch now extends at least 20 feet from the bunks that used to be protected by a wire fence to keep out the bears. A modern metal mechanism to hang food at night – up away from the bears – makes this more of a backcountry Ritz than a Hilton.

Sanctuary

The guys who walked past while I rested and wrote on Rocky Top are here, and the linear community that lives on the Appalachian Trail has convened. We've swapped stories about tough trails, inquired about places we've never been but want to go and joked about how the mountains have worn us out. But, we grin and agree that we'll keep coming back.

The linear community on the trail – but especially the AT – is amazingly efficient. So far, over the space of 15 minutes, we've verbally "googled" the best trail to take to Cades Cove, what it's like to hike the White Mountains in New Hampshire, the condition of the shelters along the AT from Clingmans Dome to Fontana Lake and discovered several options about how to best prepare Ramen noodles.

The trail log, a simple wire-bound notebook protected by a Zip-loc bag, gives a recent history of visitors to the Spence Field Hilton. This volume started on May 1, after most of the northbound through-hikers – those folks on the hike of a lifetime, tackling the 2,174 miles of the AT over the span a few months – had already passed through. Most of the entries are less than a month old.

Annie and Ben were almost done with the AT through the Smokies and planned to head to Bryson City, North Carolina, to hunt down a cheeseburger after they finished their journey. Tai celebrated his 29th birthday in the shelter. A guy who called himself an "old day hiker" wrote about how he had been at Spence on December 28, 1975, when the temperature was five degrees below zero. He said it was an easier hike at 23 than it was now that he was 56, but, he said, "Still beautiful."

Tom, Lee and Russell took a "mini man-vacation" and had "awesome fireside chats." Cowgirl and Bigfoot – lots of ATers take on trail names – said, "Great shelter. THANKS." Spritely Pixie and Caribou came in out of the weather and offered their thanks to the trail angels for a "great privy and shelter." Sharecrow scared up a wild pig on the way in before putting down for the night at Spence.

Long-distance communication is amazingly easy up here in the high country. Years ago, I was behind schedule on a long hike and needed to let my dad know I was off schedule, since he was to meet me at Newfound Gap with fresh supplies. So, I passed a note to a fellow hiker – a total stranger – who was headed out of the backcountry later that day. He called my dad when he got back to civilization and told him the new arrangements. Dad and I rendezvoused right on time.

The six of us here at the shelter right now range in age from early 30s to late 50s, from different states and different status. But we bonded immediately. Shared experiences, shared goals, similar views of life that brought us to the mountains in the first place likely aided us in easily forming an empathetic and egalitarian community. Perhaps practicality pushed us together. Here in the backcountry, all we have are the packs on our backs and each other.

Sanctuary

Four of the guys left for Cades Cove, and Paul – the senior of our group at 56 – has decided to stay the night at Spence. He says he's hiked much of the AT, but he's out here in cutoff jeans and soft-soled athletic shoes listening to a local AM radio station. Paul doesn't fit the mold one expects to find on the AT, but he climbed Thunderhead earlier in the day and that's enough bona fides for me. Hikers come in all sizes and shapes and ages, come from all professions and places, and they come to the high country for innumerable reasons and out of a myriad of motivations. All of us emptied our packs and gave Paul the food we weren't going to need.

It was here at the Spence Field Shelter years ago – before it became a Hilton – that I first learned about the mysterious Bodina. The trail logs along this section of the AT were rife with references to this mystical and mythical beauty who roamed the backcountry, and the collective quest for this goddess of the AT became the stuff of legend. As exotic as she was erotic, Bodina was the object of affection of many mountain men (and perhaps a few mountain women). Always pursued, never quite captured, the elusive Bodina, the Aphrodite of the Appalachian Trail, spurred hikers on, and the stories about her in the trail logs entertained around campfires.

Some suggested they had an Appalachian assignation with Bodina, but I don't believe them. Others reported items from their packs going missing – or items they thought they lost being found – and blamed it on Bodina. Still others said they saw her on the edges of the light from the fire pit outside the shelters, but when they went to look, only a sweetly intoxicating aroma remained at the spot where they thought they saw her standing.

Wait. I wonder? I wonder if Felice and Boudleaux Bryant, the songwriters responsible for that raucous "Rocky Top" that reverberates around Neyland Stadium in Knoxville during football games, ever came up here to the high country. I mean, the real Rocky Top is just up the Appalachian Trail. Their song says, "Once I had a girl on Rocky Top, half bear the other half cat. Wild as a mink but sweet as soda pop, I still dream about that."

Hmmm? Rocky Top? A wild, sweet girl? Bodina? Could it be?

Sanctuary

"Rocky Top, you'll always be home sweet home to me.
Good ole Rocky Top, Rocky Top, Tennessee."

Felice and Boudleaux Bryant
From "Rocky Top"

Mt. Collins Shelter

Seventeen years ago, a shelter never looked so good. I had finally finished a hellacious day on the Appalachian Trail – 15 miles including the maddening, to me, walk within earshot of Clingmans Dome Road. Today, our pace is leisurely, the road noise muffled, the quiet comforting, and Mt. Collins shelter is closed to overnight stays due to aggressive bear activity.

Collins still contains the "charm" of the shelters of old. The chain-link fence guards weary hikers from the hungry and curious bears. The fire-ring out front is lined with logs for backcountry walkers to sit on when they lie and lament around the fire. Chains still dangle from the ceiling to hang backpacks from in the ridiculous hope that mice won't gnaw on the pack in their search for food. In fact, after a few nights on the trail, the wise backpacker leaves the zippers undone so the gymnastic rodents can search the pockets of the pack without eating holes in it.

The pesky varmints kept me awake anyway on that now long-ago night. Besides being exhausted from a big-mileage day, a summer thunderstorm had roiled the mountains as it rolled across. Walking the last several miles in a torrential rain with lightning cracking all around, I had just enough strength to prepare dinner, hang my food outside the shelter high enough to keep it from the bears, hook my pack in the middle of the playground for Mickey and his friends and brush my teeth before crawling into my sleeping bag. Before I fell fast asleep, I pitched the plastic bag holding my toothbrush and toothpaste beside my bedroll.

Bad move. Being the hungry and curious little buggers they are, mice kept coming to get a taste of the toothpaste. I spent the night alternately snoring and shooing the crazy critters away.

The thunderstorm I walked through, though, carried with it an awakening. As the first grumbles of thunder rocked through the mountains, I hurriedly checked my map for places to take cover. Finding none, I quickly calculated the distance to the shelter at Mt. Collins, and somewhat sadly saw I had over an hour to go. To top it all, darkness would come earlier with the cloud cover. I was left with no alternative but to pray the storm changed direction.

It didn't. The thunder roared closer and the rains came harder. My Gore-Tex rain suit kept me mostly dry as the lightning began to rip across the sky and the thunder followed closer and closer behind the flash. Crossing a blow-down – a tree across the trail, tumbled by a previous storm – it dawned on me that I was totally unprotected on the mountain. Sure, tall trees lined the trail and would have likely caught a too-close lightning bolt first, but a falling fir could have become my guillotine.

My awareness and anxiety spiked when I felt the hair on my neck tingling – literally. With no place to hide, I realized something I hated to admit – I was helpless, totally at the mercy of nature, completely unable to control my environment. "If God doesn't protect me," I thought, "I will die." That thought – that I was a hiker in the hands of what I hoped was a benevolent God – prodded me up the trail and pushed me to prayer.

"Lord, I am helpless and hopeless without You," I cried. "Protect me, I pray." I continued, "You gave me life. Now, I give it back to You." Desperately I entreated, even though I was merely acknowledging the obvious; "Do with me as You will." Miraculously, peace came. In the midst of the storm, absolutely powerless, desperately dependent, living as close to death as I could ever remember, peace came.

Another miracle happened here on Mt. Collins a few years later. I'd hiked up Deep Creek from Bryson City and put down for the night at the head of Deep Creek when another storm blew in. The next day,

I cooked my oatmeal as raindrops spattered in it, packed up and walked up the Fork Ridge Trail toward Clingmans Dome Road.

The rains stopped about the time I hit the remnants of a snowstorm on Mt. Collins. Unprepared for hiking through snow, one step forward led to half a step back. The road to Clingmans was closed for the winter – had been for a couple of months – so there was no way to hitch a ride out to escape the weather. Weary and wet through and through, I decided to take a brief detour off the Sugarland Mountain Trail to the Mt. Collins shelter for an afternoon snack.

Some little part of the optimist in me – probably the daydreaming, delusional part – thought about a fire even though all the wood in all of the Smokies was likely wet. Plus, knowing the road to Clingmans was closed, which makes for a multi-mile hike into Mt. Collins and there's really nothing to see around it, I suspected no one had been at the shelter for a while, and I certainly didn't expect to find anything or anyone to help me once I got there.

So, I pulled into the empty shelter in hopes of just getting out of the weather for a while, shucked off my pack and stamped around the shelter a bit. Then, I saw it. Wood. Completely dry fuel for a fire. Twigs and small branches piled neatly in front of the fireplace like someone left it there just for me. I smiled at my good fortune.

Besides the waiting wood, on a flat rock above the fireplace, someone had tucked several sticks of fire-starter, the rectangular pressed-wood type laced with a small amount of accelerant that you could buy at Kmart or like you might find in a well-stocked rental cabin. And, outside in the fire ring laid several small logs, barely wet despite the rain I had been in for a day and the snowstorm that had whitened the top of the mountain.

Nobody – hardly anybody, anyway – walks through here in winter. And, why would they leave fire-starter and kindling behind? How could it possibly have been that just what I needed was waiting for me at just the time I needed it? I built my fire, warmed myself, dried my socks and marveled at the mystery. Or miracle.

The silence outside the shelter is in stark contrast to the ominous racket that followed me on my first visit here so many years ago. But, if I listen very carefully and turn my head just so, I swear I can hear the whisper I heard on this mountain in the midst of that storm: "Peace."

Sanctuary

"*The man with the knapsack is never lost. No matter whither he may stray, his food and shelter are right with him, and home is wherever he may choose to stop.*"

Horace Kephart
Author/Advocate

Newfound Gap

President Franklin Delano Roosevelt stood on this structure, the Rockefeller Memorial, on September 2, 1940, and addressed a crowd of hundreds. The 32nd president had come to the mountains to dedicate the Great Smoky Mountains National Park, and he stood and spoke from this rock tribute constructed by the Civilian Conservation Corps in honor of the mother of John D. Rockefeller, Jr., the tycoon and philanthropist who donated $5 million of the $12 million needed to establish the Park. "We meet today to dedicate the mountains, streams and forest to the service of the American people," Roosevelt said.

One has to wonder, though, even as visionary as he was, if Roosevelt could have imagined just what the Park has become. Could he have possibly foreseen the nine-plus million visitors the Smokies welcome each year? When he gazed around at the south side of Mt. LeConte and looked west toward Andrews Bald and Clingmans Dome, could he have contemplated over 800 miles of hiking trails and dozens of backcountry campsites? Did he see into the future and glimpse the development down in Gatlinburg and over in Cherokee – the good and the bad of it – and envision how the Smokies would become the economic engine that drives the lives of so many people?

FDR was the first – and so far the only – president to visit the Great Smoky Mountains National Park while in office. That's unfortunate. The needs of the most visited national park in the nation would lie unknown if not for diligent park staff and the conscientious congressional delegations of Tennessee and North Carolina. The wear and tear of millions on this Park – the one that is, as I just heard one tourist say, "almost on top of God's country" – leaves the Smokies in constant need of more money if it is to truly fulfill Roosevelt's words and continue to be of "service to the American people."

As the female tourist passing by said, this is the top of the Smokies for most who come here. With views of the waves of mountains washing away into North Carolina and a clear look at the clouds clinging to the top of Mt. LeConte, this stone vantage point turns into a bustling landmark during tourist season. Families and lovers pause for pictures while kids climb the rocks until mom or dad pulls them back down. The facilities just down an asphalt path from the memorial are heavily frequented here at the halfway point between Gatlinburg and Cherokee, and the Appalachian Trail tempts even timid tenderfoots to take a step or two toward Mt. Katahdin, 1,972 miles to the north in Maine.

This is through-hiker heaven in the summer. Running water, a real bathroom and the halfway point through the rugged Smokies, a stop at Newfound Gap adds a bit of spring to the step. And, if the backpacker is lucky, some fine fuel to the stomach.

Back in 1991, on a through-hike on the AT through the Smokies, my hiking pal and I hit Newfound early in the afternoon around the 4th of July. The parking lot was teeming with tourists marveling at the mountains and enjoying life on top. Dirty and disheveled after days on the trail, we walked off the AT and into the clean folks who'd stopped here for a while. Our smell was likely worse than our scruffy appearance and more than one mother quietly wrapped her arm around little Johnny or Janie just in case we filthy men were as unsafe as we were unkempt.

But, their curiosity eventually got the best of them. Young and old would sidle up to us, keeping a safe distance, and start to ask questions. "How far ya been?" "Where ya going?" "What do you eat out there?" "Where do you sleep?" "Where do you go to the bathroom?" "Have you seen any bears?" And on and on.

We answered questions for a while, and then it happened; we yogied them. I'd read about yogiing before. Named after everybody's favorite cartoon bear from yesteryear – Yogi the Bear – "to yogi" is to talk some unsuspecting tourist out of food. Better yet, "to yogi" is to tell such compelling stories in such a whimsical or mysterious way as to have the tourists open their picnic basket without even being asked. Like Yogi did.

Sure enough, after half an hour or so, a kindly couple well into middle age popped the trunk of their car and gave us a sandwich. Then another. And another. They gave us their Diet Pepsis and chips and almost everything else in their picnic basket. Finally, we hit the mother lode – chocolate candy bars – and the sugar rush, after days of freeze-dried carbohydrates, flew us high as a kite.

Stuffed to the point of shame, we finally said, "No more." The kind man, surely one of the trail angels who monitor the AT, even offered us money. "No thanks," we said, by now feeling a tad guilty. I asked him to call my folks when he got back to the valley and let them know I would be at Clingmans Dome by noon the next day and that they could meet me there. Mother told me later that the man who called her was so nice and went on and on about our encounter at Newfound.

A plaque on the monument here at Newfound Gap that says the Park is "for the permanent enjoyment of the people" got it exactly right. Children race up the steps and yell back down to their parents, "Look, we can see the clouds," while they point at Mt. LeConte. A mother kindly asks my wife, Diane, to take a picture of her family of four. Grown men and women turn a tad childlike as they peer out at the same view FDR looked at almost 70 years ago. Couples cuddle up on the edge of the memorial and have perfect strangers snap a photo to make a memory in the mountains.

The western ridges are glowing pink and the temperature has dropped with the sun on this fall afternoon. The parking lot is emptying, the people satiated by a sumptuous serving of the Smokies, just as Roosevelt intended.

"If future generations are to remember us with gratitude rather than contempt, we must leave them more than the miracles of technology. We must leave them a glimpse of the world as it was in the beginning, not just after we got through with it."

President Lyndon B. Johnson
Upon signing the Wilderness Act of 1964

Rainbow Falls

    The afternoon sun chased me up the trail, causing the woods to cast an eastern shadow and awakening the elfish nature of this old, second-growth forest. The woodlands just above the trailhead are open, free of undergrowth, with room for light to dance to the tune of the trickle of the stream. Even here at the falls, this 80-foot ribbon of water, the late light shines up the valley, sheens off the rhododendron leaves and bathes the falls near the end of today.
    The woods have a different feel in the afternoon. They move me differently as well. With day dying, my hike became a hump, my pace quickened by the coming sunset. I missed my uphill hike last weekend, and my legs and lungs and heart let me know it was time to go to the woods again. My schedule was awful, my time too short. Still, I had to come.

Sanctuary

The Dow Jones Industrial Average was down over 300 points today, Congress is in the process of passing a $700-billion rescue plan – which may or may not work – in hopes of pulling the economy out of its most tenuous and frightening situation in 75 years and tonight the candidates for vice president of the United States debate. Doom and gloom are about in the land. So, I came to the woods and walked with the sunshine at my back.

Down below, I passed the place I brought the kids while my girls were still toddling. We came and threw rocks into LeConte Creek and hiked a few hundred yards up the trail. I showed them the mini-ecosystem emerging from a long-fallen log – the moss, the lichens, the flowers – and explained to them how that tree lived and died and now new life was coming from it even in death. They asked to go throw more rocks.

The way here was distinctly different in the afternoon. The sun soothed as it ducked and darted between the leaves. Parts of the trail were already darkening when the path bent around a mountain or tucked behind a ridge. The sun seemed to already be setting as it sunk toward tree line, only to reappear burning brightly when I rounded a bend and had a western exposure.

I walked fast, pushed by the nagging knowledge that sunset will come quickly and prodded by the thought that I was walking toward the darkness. Or, at least racing it, trying to make it to my destination and snap some photos, put the pen to the page and make it back down the rocky trail before night finally falls. Not that I fear the darkness. I've a flashlight in my pack, and I've night-hiked before. Still, the thought of darkness moved me on.

Maybe we all walk with trepidation toward the darkness. Having worked with retirees for over 20 years, I've noticed many and varied reactions as time ticks on. The thought of the final darkness, for some, sends them scurrying quickly to get done those things they always intended to do. They don't let their birth certificate cast a cloud over their latter days. Sadly, though, some simply sit down and wait for the sunset of life, and the darkness creeps closer until it covers them well before the light of life actually goes out. So sad.

A mountain man of the Bible didn't let the long shadows of his last years dampen his enthusiasm. As a younger man – 40 years old, actually – Caleb was one of the twelve spies Moses sent to explore the Promised Land. Ten spies, terrified by the "giants" they saw in Canaan, forecast doom and gloom after their foray into the land God had promised to give to the Israelites hundreds of years before. But, Caleb and Joshua came back with a good report, seeing possibilities, not problems.

Caleb was promised, for his faithful service, some hill country when the Israelites first found the land intended for them. Unfortunately, it would be four decades before he saw it again. The Israelites believed the bad news, rejected the good and then wandered in the wilderness for 40 years. Caleb, though he had ample opportunity, didn't grumble about the missed opportunity, didn't complain about how much of his life had been wasted because of the foolish actions of others.

Finally, after those long years in the wilderness, the Israelites entered the Promised Land under Joshua's leadership. No sooner had the victory been won than Caleb reminded his old friend of the promise made to him 40 years earlier. At over 80 years old, with no hesitation, Caleb ambled up to Joshua and said, in essence, "I'm as vigorous as I was 40 years ago. I've done what God told me. Now, give me my mountain."

As the sunset of life came closer, Caleb remembered the vision of his youth. He had a purpose, a plan, a mountain to climb, something to lean into. Caleb saw his life as part of something greater than himself – fulfilling the promises of God – and refused to consign himself to a rocking chair on the front porch and hitting the early-bird specials at the nearby buffets.

The Bible says Caleb "had a different spirit about him." That different spirit is what I see in those retirees who don't let the gathering darkness, with the seemingly eternal sunshine of youth long gone and the searing sun of middle age past, send them into a dusky indifference toward life or the debilitation of depression. They're the ones who keep walking, keep climbing, keep going, even as their bodies tell them they can't. They walk toward the darkness, vigorous, alive, unafraid, always intent on possessing the mountaintop of their lives.

The last light of this day is coming closer now. Almost miraculously, the sunshine comes straight up the valley, hitting my page perfectly even as the thermometer drops to let me know night is nigh. Up on the falls, an autumn afternoon's spotlight illumines the moss-covered point where the waters escape from the pool on top of the cliff and spill over the rocks.

Perfect. The light is perfect on the page, on the falls and is still strong enough to put any thought of darkness completely from my mind. Regardless of when the sun sets, today left enough light to get me home.

Sanctuary

"We do not quit playing because we grow old; we grow old because we quit playing."

Oliver Wendell Holmes

Albright Grove

I mean no harm. Really. Yet, as soon as I walked around the National Park Service gate onto the Maddron Bald Trail, the watchers of the woods began to alert me that I was entering a sacred place. Staccato squawks said, "I see you!" as the shadows of the lookouts dipped and darted overhead. Threatening trills warned me to give reverence as I entered the hushed hardwoods. Crows cawed down to me, cautioning me to respect their place.

Little boomer squirrels barked, agitated that I'd interrupted their gathering, then barked again to tell me to stay on the trail where I belong and keep moving. Like on a previous visit to Albright Grove years ago, an owl roused in daylight and hooted at me, giving me a start, before flapping away as if to report my presence to the lord of this wood. Up at the Grove, his wise friend asked, "Who? Who?" as another boomer barked bravely.

"It's just me," I almost said aloud. "I come in peace."

Albright is a stately place, hardwoods and conifers rising majestically, filtering the light just right, inviting the visitor to gawk upward in this cathedral for the soul. Unlike the forest down below, this grove is dense, new growth mingled with old, with some of the deciduous sentries standing on their moss-covered roots, ready to walk away, it seems, if threatened by an unwanted intruder or prepared to step onto the trail to block the way of an unworthy interloper.

If the breathtaking panoramas of the balds of the Smokies expand the mind by showing the wideness of the wilderness, Albright urges intimacy, inviting outsiders to come and sit and stare and savor the silence. If peaks like Chimney Tops and Thunderhead beg to be climbed and flush the hiker with endorphins, Albright serves up serotonin, naturally mellowing the backwoods meanderer. And, if some of the high points in the high country quickly give travelers a vibrant vista, Albright is meant to be felt, to be pondered.

This grove is home to old growth, huge tuliptrees and remnants of their contemporaries. It's easy to forget, for us who come today, that much of the land now in the Great Smoky Mountains National Park was heavily logged. Champion Fibre Company owned this section of the park before it was purchased to be preserved. For many, nostalgia nudges us toward the cabins of the settlers, like the Baxter place back down the trail, and we hold a romanticized version of history in our head of family farms being sold – or taken – to make way for the Park. Some were. But the bulk of the mountains are blanketed by secondary growth, the virgin timber felled by farmers and logging companies alike, leaving the forests only as old as the time the axes went still and the saws stopped singing from the mountainside.

Like the woodlands, the trail to Albright turns from new to old; the early part an easy walk on an old graveled roadbed before turning into a traditional mountain footpath. Yet, even the walkway seems different as Albright comes closer with the roots and rocks on the trail covered by moss, announcing the ancient and telling travelers this is not a well-worn way.

Albright's old growth holds hints of what used to be. Tuliptrees, maples and hemlocks rise as giants here, the largest a monster over 20 feet in circumference. Up near the end of the Albright Grove Loop, a huge, still-standing log, its years of vigorous growth long gone, harkens back to a time before the loggers came. Beside it, joined to it actually, a fully mature hardwood grows strong and tall. What was stands beside what is and causes me to wonder what might have been.

What would these woods look like if the loggers never came? Would these hills and hollows be populated by giant tulip poplars and heaven-touching hemlocks? Would the chestnut blight have bypassed the Smokies instead of decimating it? Would the thickets be thinner if a higher canopy caught more of the rainwater?

What would have happened if the national park had never come? Would these mountains be barren, denuded for dollars? Would houses be hanging from every outcropping? Would the towns down below be but backwater burgs begging for jobs and commerce in a now-global economy?

Like the twinned trees in Albright, what was anchors us to our ancestors, grounds us in our genealogy. In our own lives, what was instructs and informs us as we live the what is of today. Just as the new growth is connected to the old here in the Grove, life today grew out of life that came before, the life that roots us to our place and our people. For us to grow true and tall, what was must be examined before new growth can come. But exploring what was comes at a cost. At least for me.

The what was of my life, I must confess, occupied far too much of my mind for far too long. My mulling started, not surprisingly, about the time I started coming to the mountains those now-many years ago. Devastated by divorce, my moorings were destroyed. What I had, what I hoped for, what I dreamed of disappeared. Who I was – my relationships, my occupation, my reputation, my avocation – stayed stagnant, locked in a time-warp, an old tree planted in my mind that died a slow death as I stood and watched.

What is, though, began to grow even as what was began to wither. Almost imperceptibly, this new life I live right now sprouted, grew, budded, bloomed and began to bear fruit almost unseen by me. I was too busy ruing what was, wishing and futilely hoping it would survive and wondering, over and over and over, what might have been to notice the new. Now, just now, actually, I can finally see the two trees clearly – what was and what is – and only occasionally wonder, finally without anxiety, what might have been.

Sometimes, it seems, what was, if we ponder it too long, serves as a signpost, directing us down a path to a parallel place, an unreal place, where we live in a world obsessed by what might have been. Perhaps lasting growth can only come when we acknowledge what was, release what might have been and fully recognize and embrace what is. Maybe then we are finally and fully prepared to face what will be.

The woods are quiet, the watchers apparently convinced I'm no menace to them or their calm cathedral. Indian Camp Creek's raucous roar is muffled by the undergrowth as Albright serenely lives another day, the old and the new at peace, side by side.

Sanctuary

"It is not so much for its beauty that the forest makes a claim upon men's hearts, as for that subtle something, that quality of air, that emanation from old trees, that so wonderfully changes and renews a weary spirit."

Robert Louis Stevenson

Mt. Cammerer

"Walk toward the sky." Low Gap is a lie and the trail a liar. Yes, the low end of Low Gap Trail winds through fairy-tale forest, across creeks full of moss-topped rocks and past plots that probably were planted with corn and such by the settlers here over 75 years ago. But, half a mile in on the shortest approach to Mt. Cammerer, the trail turns up and never relents for 2.5 miles.

"Walk toward the sky." The woods change as the trail steepens. Airy old-growth awash with wind rushing through the roof of the forest gives way to thickets further up the mountain. While gray squirrels darted down below near the Cosby Campground, the higher country is home to their red cousins, little boomers, ducking and hiding while giggling at a hiker huffing and puffing up the Low Gap Trail on his way to Cammerer.

"Walk toward the sky." I always seem to struggle up Low Gap. Maybe I just happen to hit it when I'm unrested. Perhaps the unnecessary anxiety beforehand intimidates me, causing me to struggle more than I ought. It could be that Low Gap Trail is just steep, an elevation gain of over 2,000 feet over the 2.5 miles, compared to a rise of 1,300 feet over two miles at the Chimney Tops. Regardless, up toward the top, I heard the trees groan, literally, as the winds gently swayed them, whether in sympathy or mockery, I do not know.

My mantra – Or was it a message from on high? – worked even as the falling acorns bounced off the bill of my cap and tapped my shoulder. The sky came and went as the trail turned away from Cosby Creek and switched back and forth, bending east before turning back west, as I labored up the diabolically deceptively named trail, the sorrily named sadist exacting its pleasure as I stepped over each root and rock.

I must admit, the past week was exhausting. The stock market had its worst week ever – worse than during the Great Depression – and my clients were concerned. Actually, they were stunned, frightened, panicked, frantic. Wife Diane and I made a quick trip to Nashville for me to cover the presidential debate at Belmont University. Somehow I turned out five pieces of journalism on deadline Monday and Tuesday and hurried back to battle the fear of the Dow Jones Industrial Average's freefall. Thankfully, my tormentor of a trail mercifully sweated the stress out of me.

Low Gap Trail finally ended with a flat whimper at the Appalachian Trail, less than a mile from Cosby Knob Shelter and 2.4 miles from Camel Gap. My mind raced back to my AT hike through the Smokies and my first night on the trail. Over-anxious and over-confident, I walked past the Cosby Knob Shelter, foolishly headed to Tricorner Knob. Darkness came as my water ran out, so I quickly and quietly camped at Camel Gap. Then a storm blew in on the north side of the mountain. Torrents lashed my tarp as lightning cracked nearby. Making a novice mistake, I had put down in a low spot. My camp flooded and my day of making every backcountry mistake known to humankind – my pack too heavy, my plans too heady, overreaching and underperforming – came to a humiliating end, with me the wiser for it.

I made my approach to Cammerer on that long-ago hike up the other side of the mountain on the Appalachian Trail, starting down at Davenport Gap. It's an equally hellish walk, with an elevation gain of almost 3,000 feet over about five miles. The switchbacks were just as relentless, the hike equally frustrating as horses came up and down the trail – one of the places they're allowed on the AT – their riders immune from bribes to take me to the top. Progress could be maddeningly measured against a huge water tank down in the valley near the Waterville exit off Interstate 40.

Sanctuary

When the trees along the trail finally yielded a view today, reds and yellows and rusts colored Cammerer, the mountain accented by evergreens and outlined by an always-green heath bald running up a ridge toward the top of the mountain. The perfect blue sky speckled with high white clouds seemed to smile on the mountain and grin down at me. Higher up the trail, brilliant blue backdropped a stand of trees, with me looking out at eye-level on the sky I'd been walking toward.

Now I sit in the sky on a rock outcropping just down from the Mt. Cammerer Lookout. The Lookout served as a fire-watch station from the 1930s to 1960s. Planned and constructed during the term of Arno Cammerer as director of the National Park Service on the mountain formerly known as White Rock, the octagonal icon was built by the Civilian Conservation Corps, fell into disrepair after modern fire detection techniques left it obsolete and was restored in the 1990s by Friends of the Great Smoky Mountains National Park.

The Lookout is interesting, but the view is astounding. Mt. Guyot and Mt. Sequoyah to the east, Webb Mountain and English Mountain to the north, Cocke County down below and Mt. Sterling and the ocean of mountains to the south are all vibrantly visible today after rains this week cleared the air. The wind is crisp but not chilling, sending the trees waving and cooling me from the plenty-strong autumn sun of the high country. The few clouds cast splotches of shadow on the valley and the surrounding mountains, their shapes changing as the clouds morph and the sun shifts, darkening here, lightening there.

The Lookout has turned into Grand Central Station. Due to a late start this morning, I met two hikers already on their way down on my way up. They'd come early to Cammerer to photograph the sunrise. One member of a hiking club caught up with me at the intersection of Low Gap Trail with the AT. Families are here, some with young kids, enjoying an amazing view and perfect weather. I wonder if they know. I wonder if they realize just how lucky – no, how blessed – they are to be in the high country after the rains, with visibility higher than normal and the view so expansive.

Here on Cammerer, the eastern bookend of the Great Smoky Mountains National Park, out on this point, firewatchers could see in all directions. Now, hikers come, their reward a 360-degree awe-inspiring, soul-stirring, spirit-lifting panorama, with winds to whisk away the worries of the world below and wash away the week that was. On days like today, after a hard hike up Low Gap and a run along the ridge on the Appalachian Trail, Cammerer offers an indescribable vista, beckoning backcountry lovers to bask in the beauty as the sun caresses them while they tilt their faces upward to kiss the sky.

Sanctuary

"Climb the mountains and get their good tidings. Nature's peace will flow into you as sunshine flows into trees. The winds will blow their own freshness into you... while cares will drop off like autumn leaves."

John Muir

Abrams Falls

The Sabbath broke crystal-clear on Cades Cove, with Thunderhead Mountain and Gregory Bald, the big backdrops for the western end of the Smokies, catching the first rays of day while the eastern ridges of the mountains filtered a perfect sunrise across the valley. Fog hung low and young deer danced as they grazed, frolicking for photos by the tourists arriving just after daybreak. The walk in to Abrams Falls was everything the climb up Low Gap to Mt. Cammerer a day ago was not.

Abrams Falls Trail undulates gently beside Abrams Creek, the trail a wide footpath that feels like a boulevard compared to some of the narrow ways in the backcountry. The trail, unlike the lying Low Gap Trail and so many others, is relatively root and rock free with long, flat sections that let a hiker walk with his head up, enjoying the scenery and serenity while watching the early sun cut through the canopy as it follows the creek toward the falls.

It's possible, on Abrams trail, to let the mind go, this easy path removing the worry of stumbling over a rock or root and the need to concentrate on a hard uphill push. Walking, putting one foot down then picking up the other, becomes autonomic, an unthinking action that occupies enough of the body to let the mind roam free, uninterrupted by having to pick the best route up and over rugged sections of trail. The ripples and roars of the close-by creek massage the soul and the flitting and flickering sunshine spotlights autumn's colors in the forest.

A few leafdrops of fall rained down on the trail, twisting and turning as they drifted downward on an easy wind. Autumn is here. Colors were more pronounced yesterday up high on the crest of Cammerer, but the creek banks along Abrams are nicely gold and crimson and copper with the evergreens providing radiant relief. The peak of this season's color will be coming soon.

It's a bit strange to be here on a Sunday, I guess. Our church, Apostles Anglican, has become our Sunday home, a place where our spirits are refreshed and our souls restored. We're strengthened there, by the worship, the liturgy, the Word and the Eucharist. The old of Anglicanism and the new of Celtic worship songs are the perfect blend for us. Grace abounds, enough that I don't feel an iota of guilt about coming to Abrams to worship in a different way.

The metaphors are many on the tranquil walk to the falls. The living water flowing past on the way in and here at the falls calmed me and cleansed my heart and mind. The light on the world around me sent pleasing sensations through my soul. I stood on the rock in the middle of the strong current to snap photos, my feet secure, my spirit sure. Every sound is a psalm, every view a hymn, every step a sermon, the whole hike a liturgy drawing my heart toward heaven.

I do not write of pantheism. The mountains, in all their intricacy and glory, could not have come from some cosmic coincidence or heavenly happenstance. Rather, out here in the midst of Creation, away from human-engineered contraptions, God's handiwork is observable, His craftsmanship close by, His Presence evident in every sight and sound. "Praise the LORD, O my soul," the psalmist wrote. "O Lord my God, You are very great; You are clothed with splendor and majesty." So is His place.

On these quiet paths like Abrams Falls Trail, we can hear His whisper. Yesterday, on top of Cammerer, the vista was so expansive, so amazing, one stuttered and stammered to even describe it. The magnificence of the moment, up high, closer to the seat of God it seemed, overwhelmed my limited intellect and inadequate vocabulary. I could only marvel at the majesty, His majesty, and somewhat incoherently mutter my amazement at the blessing of His beauty.

Here, though, on this quiet walk, through His hushed and holy wood, the mind is free to contemplate, to consider, to ask and to answer in an intensely intimate way. Like Elijah hidden in the mountain after a contentious conflagration with the enemies of Jehovah, here on this rock, surrounded by old logs and rhododendron and hardwoods, with the roar of the falls muting the voices of the others who have come, I can hear the still small voice speaking from the whisper of the wind of the Holy Spirit. The voice of God, speaking affirmation, offering correction, gently convicting, patiently instructing, lovingly guiding, comes quietly in these mountains to those who have ears to hear.

On this holiday weekend with colors coming to the mountains and the weather fair, people come and go from the falls. Some climb up to the top. Others walk in, pose, snap a photo and are gone. A few sit and snack and talk for awhile. Then, they're off. Too often, I think, I've done the same here in the Smokies. Walk fast. Climb high. Get the photo. Get back to the outside world to show people where I've been, what I've seen, what I've done.

Sadly, I'm afraid I've done the same in my worship of the Maker of the mountains, going for the glorious, marveling at the majestic, making quick work of my worship. Go to church. Sing the songs. Climb to an emotional peak. Snap a photo in my mind. Sit and snack on the sacrament. Then, I'm off, back into the world, carrying only souvenirs from the sanctuary and the crumbs of communion.

But, here today, I have lingered, waiting quietly in this gorgeous place for the whisper of God as I sat on the rock, let the living water rush past and watched the light paint this part of the world. The wind stirs, brushing by and sending leaves tumbling. Earlier, as I snapped my own photos of the falls, a gust up high sent a shower of leaves falling over me. They drifted and twisted in front of me before calmly collecting on the surface of the pool below the falls, bobbing and swaying to a mystical rhythm all their own.

Sanctuary

"For in the true nature of things, if we rightly consider, every green tree is far more glorious than if it were made of gold and silver."

Martin Luther

Cades Cove

So much for solitude. Cades Cove is crawling with tourists, an irresistible autumn Sunday drawing car hikers and windshield adventurers into the outdoors to grab a glimpse of the Smokies while laying hold of a hint of history. The line of vehicles began at the gate to Cades Cove just after daybreak, the early arrivals mesmerized by horses grazing in the field, the spindly-legged deer roaming free and the comforting shadows of the magic hour after sunrise.

Hours later, I'm in the Dan Lawson place, sitting upstairs in the room where the kids probably slept as the wind rattled around the solitary window. Even though Dan and friends carefully constructed this cabin in 1856, the cracks in the walls likely couldn't keep out the cold on a winter's night. Cades Cove contains nuggets of nostalgia – cabins like this as well as John Cable's grist mill and numerous churches and other structures – to give visitors a feel for life in the 19th and early-20th centuries.

The traffic in the Cove, though, is totally modern, with more flashing brake lights and stops and starts than Manhattan at rush hour. Though signs beg motorists not to stop in the road, deer wandering in the meadows cause even the most compliant traveler to slow to a crawl and watch. Back up the road a bit, two big-racked bucks foraged in the forest and cars were pulling off the road in all directions, their occupants sprinting through the traffic to get back and see the deer, creating a scene as frenetic as a NASCAR pit stop.

Over nine million people visit the Great Smoky Mountains National Park every year, and in spring and autumn, it seems they're all here on the Cades Cove Loop. Young and old and in between look and point and pull over to explore the cabins and barns and smokehouses while they stare up at the mountains. The Cable Mill area is a favorite stop. Besides the facilities that almost every car needs at the halfway point on the Loop, the mill is preserved on its original location, a cantilever barn shows off old farm implements and a sorghum mill sits in front of the Gregg-Cable House.

The traffic in the Cove can be frustrating, but no more so than an event that didn't happen back in 2005. President George W. Bush scheduled an Earth Day visit to the Smokies and was supposed to speak from a podium constructed in a field here in Cades Cove. I applied for press credentials to cover the historic event; Bush would have been the first sitting president since Franklin Roosevelt to visit the Great Smoky Mountains National Park.

The credentialing process was maddeningly detailed, the White House selective, the Secret Service, well, secretive, as well as humorless. Being relatively new to journalism, my hopes weren't high, given the number of larger publications coming to cover the event and the bigger-name journalists vying for admission.

A friend's husband worked at the Park Service and was involved in preparations. She told me how plans kept changing and how the D.C. bureaucracy caused work days to be delayed, meaning her husband ended up putting in odd, long, late hours. The possibility of a presidential visit, though, had every lover of the Smokies going over and above to prepare and spiff up the perfection of this corner of God's Creation.

The day came for Bush's visit, and I came to Cades Cove with only a letter from my editor saying I was who I said I was, since I was to pick up my credentials on site. At the first checkpoint, all the way back in Townsend, a Tennessee state trooper looked skeptically at my letter before waving me on through, trusting the Secret Service would nab me if I was lying. Park personnel routed journalists and political attendees through what is normally the exit to Cades Cove Loop, funneling everyone to the Cable Mill area. I breathed a sigh of relief when my White House press pass was there.

Rainclouds gathered and released a few drops as we wandered the parking lot and waited. I got a chance to speak to my friend's husband, and he filled me in on his own frustration at the constantly changing instructions from Washington. Shortly, a deluge drove us back to our vehicles, where we waited out the storm. The weather finally broke in the Cove, but storm clouds still hovered over the mountain tops.

Finally, the call came for the press and politicos to board the bus to go to the site of Bush's speech. We rode halfway around the Cove, spotting Secret Service agents in yellow rain slickers tromping through the woods to secure the area. Mounted law enforcement patrolled the perimeter as our bus came to a stop and the door opened.

"Event's cancelled, folks," the Park Service spokesman said. The bus full of reporters and political types stared at him, stunned to silence. He told us the storms had settled over McGhee Tyson Airport, where Air Force One had landed, and the bad weather had grounded the helicopter that was to bring the president to the Park.

Our bus made its way back to the Cable Mill area, I disembarked and climbed in my car to listen to Bush's speech, the one I was supposed to witness, being delivered in an airport hangar and broadcast over the radio. As he spoke, the rain stopped and Cades Cove began to clear of clouds and traffic.

Bush's speech wasn't memorable. Neither was the column I wrote about it. But, as I drove out of the Cove in bumper-to-bumper traffic, my agitation gave way to wonder. Fine filaments of clouds came up from the valley and climbed the ridgelines toward the crest, flying through the folds in the mountains, whisking away the weather and my frustration. As unmemorable as the day turned out, I do remember the last line of the column I wrote about it;

"There's never a bad day in Cades Cove."

"What a joy it is to feel the soft, springy earth under my feet once more, to follow grassy roads that lead to ferny brooks where I can bathe my fingers in a cataract of rippling notes, or to clamber over a stone wall into green fields that tumble and roll and climb in riotous gladness!"

Helen Keller

Laurel Falls

Sanctuary, I suppose, does not require solitude nor can it only be found behind the green gates and walls of wilderness that guard the deep places of the Great Smoky Mountains. Dozens of folks have found it here today at Laurel Falls, only a 1.3-mile walk from the parking lot on Little River Road.

Sanctuary is not dependent on ruggedness or difficulty. The path here is paved with old asphalt, uneven in spots, tilting in places, but smooth enough to allow access by wheelchairs and baby strollers that carry their passengers through the woods to this 40-foot falls. The trail winds through friendly forest, the colors of fall brushed dusky this afternoon by the setting autumn sun.

If I remember correctly, we brought my twin daughters here, Haley and Micah, in their tandem buggy with big tires when they were too small to walk the whole way. They escaped their carriage and bounced around the pool below the falls as their adult chaperones carefully, and nervously, kept them away from the edge of a 30-foot cliff that gives the stream another ledge over which to tumble.

Laurel Falls is a family place; young, old, middle-aged, short, tall, thin and not so thin were on the trail either coming or going as I walked in after work this afternoon. My dad brought my son, Reed, here for Reed's first hike. Somewhere there's a photo of Reed splashing in the pool at the foot of the falls. Where the photo is now I have no idea, but the image of a boy and his grandfather cavorting on the rocks at the bottom of a waterfall in the Smokies is etched eternally in my mind.

Sanctuary implies a place of protection and it is that, I guess. In the time of St. Benedict, travelers sought protection from the rogues of the road in the sanctuary behind the walls of monasteries. But sanctuary is also a place of escape – escape from the world and its worries, escape from the hurry of humanity and the sameness of society. The Smokies offer a place to escape our lives in boxes, as a minister friend once described our everyday existence.

We wake up in the box of our bedroom inside the box of our house, move to the box of our vehicle and, for many of us, move to the box of our office. And, in today's world, we turn on the box of our computer to stare into the box of its monitor for eight hours at work before hustling home to watch a box filled with baseball or football or politics or cooking shows. Or, if we're adventurous, we change the box to a channel to watch a show about people who have escaped the box to experience the great outdoors.

Laurel Falls is running steadily, filling its pool before releasing the stream through four of the six culverts that pass under a bridge where it pools again before dropping over the edge of the cliff where I sit. I'm almost alone now as the sun has ducked down behind a ridge, taking the temperature with it, making me glad for the sweatshirt that was too hot on the way in. A steady stream of hikers has already exited, including a couple of contemplatives who were here earlier. They had drawn back away from the falls to solitary spots on the side of the mountain – one reading, the other writing – absorbed in their own worlds. They found sanctuary.

I did a night hike here once. Frustrated and frazzled, I needed to escape from the whirl of uncertainty in the valley. As I stepped into the darkness and onto the trail, I prayed for moonlight but none came. I walked most of the way with my torch trained on the trail. Night sounds echoed through the forest, amplified by the stillness and, to be honest, my apprehension of what the night might bring.

When I arrived at the falls, the roar masked the cheeps and creaks and calls of the night, and the waters danced oddly in my artificial light. I steered clear of the cliff and ended up leaning against the wooden handrails on the concrete bridge below the falls. My skittishness was gone, and I turned off the torch.

Pitch blackness enveloped me on that starless night, wrapping me in a somewhat surreal cocoon of calm. As the water tumbled, my frustrations went with it, and my former frenzy dissipated. In the wild at night, serenity found me, drew me close and flung its cloak of comfort around me. Darkness, rather than light, brought a sense of security.

Maybe that's what sanctuary really is: a place we can find serenity, security and safety, where we are hidden from the things – even those within us – that haunt us, that hunt us, that want to do us harm. Perhaps sanctuary is found not behind fortified walls and locked doors, like in the monastic days of old, but rather it is found in that place where we can open ourselves up, unlock those things we've kept closed up inside of us and tear down the walls that separate us from God and others.

Sanctuary is that place where we can forgo vigilance, stop guarding our persona, our position, our prestige and laugh at silly jokes, cry because we need to, say what is on our minds, reveal what is in our hearts and put away all pretense. We can, as trite as it might sound, be who we are, unafraid of rejection or judgment or ridicule, from ourselves as much as others. Sanctuary is a place of grace, where unmerited and unconditional love flows freely, where acceptance is unquestioned and affirmation comes quickly and often.

Darkness is upon me, and I can already feel the cloak of calm coming. Is it the stillness of the Smokies that brings the serenity? Is it possible, in some strange irony, that out here in the wilderness we leave behind our boxes and find security in the wild? Or, is it the unfiltered closeness to Creation, the easily observable evidence of God that makes us feel safe?

Perhaps sanctuary is the sum of them all.

Sanctuary

"*For we need this thing wilderness far more than it needs us. Civilizations (like glaciers) come and go, but the mountain and its forest continue the course of creation's destiny. And in this we mere humans can take part – by fitting our civilization to the mountain.*"

Benton MacKaye
Originator of the idea for the Appalachian Trail

Porters Creek

Maybe this is my cabin for crisis. The Smoky Mountain Hiking Club cabin, built in 1934-1936, is one mile in on the Porters Creek Trail. The easy walk on the graveled road that is this trail has brought me here numerous times. I've come here with my kids – a photo on our wall at home shows Haley and Micah pensively holding the posts on the front porch of the cabin while Reed mugs for the camera – and I've trooped up here with church groups of adults and teenagers.

But, like today, I've come here alone several times. Perhaps it's the white noise of the creek that calls me up into this cove. It could be the historicity of the area. Stacked stones mark former home places along the trail. My paternal grandmother's people came from this area of the Smokies and maybe some mysterious, almost mystical attraction of ancestry draws me. An old cemetery rests along the path. At the one-mile mark, where the road loops around for National Park Service vehicles to come bringing men to do maintenance, the John Messer Barn stands just a few yards off the trail. Built in 1876, the cantilever barn possibly transports me back to an earlier, simpler time. A few steps and across a creek from the barn, a sturdy log springhouse with a shake roof still protects the water supply.

The cabin stands solidly just past the springhouse, the chinking firmly in place. The stone porch has an inviting wooden bench and, inside, the southern room of the two-room cabin has wire-mesh bunks where hikers used to bed down before the Park Service closed the area to campers. Stone steps a few feet in front of the porch lead away from the cabin and up the hill toward where a structure used to be. Curiously, the yard is littered with three old millstones, one a quarter covered with moss, another set in the stone walkway in front of the cabin and the third up the mountain a bit from the cabin, all of them now blended beautifully into the landscape.

A group of school kids was leaving just as I arrived, their adult minders apologizing for the kids' enthusiasm, telling me they hoped I didn't come to photograph wildlife because the children had surely scared any deer away. A few years back, before I hiked with a camera on my hip, a nice sized doe met me at the barn as I left the cabin to head home. She stared at me and I stared at her until she finally lost interest and wandered into the woods. Maybe she was hoping for food.

The Porters Creek Trail continues on along the creek from here, changing from a roadbed to a regular trail, for 2.7 miles to a backcountry campsite. The campsite is closed right now due to aggressive bear activity, but, years ago, the campsite served as a staging area for my climb up the Porters Creek manway to the Appalachian Trail.

Sanctuary

The Brushy Mountain Trail leaves from the loop at the end of the graveled road and crosses Brushy Mountain before intersecting with the Trillium Gap Trail that turns up Mt. LeConte toward the lodge and down to Grotto Falls. I've never walked up Brushy, but my folks went that way once. Some friends told me about running upon some bears on Brushy. The bears moved on and so did my friends.

The woods are changing colors quickly now, with the yard of the cabin littered with foliage that has already done its artistic duty for the year. Occasionally, another leaf lets go of its limb and quickly wafts to the ground. Specks of rain drop onto the walkway, proving my wife right on her admonition to bring a raincoat.

I was here on a rainy January day in 1995, chased to the mountains by the cares of the world. I picked Porters because the hike is quick and the cabin is dry, my need then more for meditation than for exercise. To be honest, I can't remember what the crisis was that pushed me up Porters. Family or work or conflict or theological angst or maybe all of the above caused me to need a quiet place to contemplate, to pray, to rest.

I tried to start a fire in the fireplace in the cabin but none lasted long. The wood was too wet and there wasn't enough, so I finally gave up and put on my rain suit to trap my body's heat and keep the wet, winter cold away. Eventually, in my exhaustion from carrying the millstones of my problems for days or weeks or months, I stretched out on a wire bunk and slept for a while. Fitfully. But, I slept.

There was no milestone moment when my millstones fell away. But, after spending a morning here doing nothing but listening to the rain, praying, eating, reading Scripture and sleeping, I walked out lighter, my load lifted by my time in the woods.

The crisis I come from today is definable, observable, inescapable. For the past month, economic fear, and sometimes outright panic, has gripped the globe. The bursting of the housing bubble of the mid-2000s has set off a chain of events that has caused banks to stop lending and borrowers to stop borrowing, leading prognosticators and pundits to warn of another Great Depression.

The stock market, from which I earn my livelihood, was down almost 40 percent year-to-date through yesterday. The month of October has, so far, seen stock prices plummet precipitously. Good companies – blue chips, we call them – are trading at half or a third of what their prices were only a few months ago.

But, the real crisis is for those investors who depend on their investments for income in retirement. The carnage has come so quickly and has cut their investments so deeply, some – only some, thankfully – may have to lower their income and even their standard of living. Some younger folks may have to delay retirement. There is a human toll to the greed of all parties involved in inflating the housing bubble, and their avarice has caused responsible, financially conservative people to pay a price for the errors of others.

Every day at work for the past month, I've felt like a surgeon in an emergency room on a battlefield near the front lines. More bad news comes, the markets crater, then rise, then drop again. Clients call and are concerned. I call clients and address their concerns. Other clients call and express their concern for me.

Today, though, was the first day I felt myself start to crack. Several crises this morning led to debilitation by noon. I fortified with an open-faced roast beef sandwich at lunch and went back to the fray, finished work by 4:00 p.m. and hiked up to here.

I felt the darkness of despair drawing ominously closer earlier today. Now, night is descending on this farm site on Porters Creek. But, after walking this short way, praying and just sitting quietly on the front porch of my cabin for crisis, my millstones are gone and the shadows have been chased from my soul.

Sanctuary

"By reading the scriptures I am so renewed that all nature seems renewed around me and with me. The sky seems to be a pure, a cooler blue, the trees a deeper green. The whole world is charged with the glory of God and I feel fire and music under my feet."

Thomas Merton

Mt. LeConte
Alum Cave Trail

Exhaustion and traffic put me behind plan on the last leg of this two-and-a-half month journey. It was another week that was at work – wild gyrations in the stock market, excruciatingly bad economic news, another presidential debate in an amped-up election season – and I simply couldn't kick-start myself out the door any earlier than noon. Diane urged me on – "You'll be miserable if you just stay here and watch football." – and son Reed turned the tables on me over the phone. "You'll love it once you get out there, Dad," he said.

Traffic was terrible into Gatlinburg, edging along a little at a time, the leaf seekers headed to the mountains in hopes of catching a peek at peak colors in the Park, I guessed. But, when I veered off the Parkway onto the Gatlinburg By-Pass, the road was manageable with only the occasional sudden stop or frantic left turn into an overlook to catch a glimpse down into Gatlinburg or up to LeConte.

I grinned. Mt. LeConte had color enough down low, but only a third or maybe a half of the mountain was visible, the rest covered by what weather forecasters called a partly cloudy day. Down at home, the rains had moved on and the remnants of clouds were quickly following. But LeConte had captured some of the stragglers and was still holding on to them tightly.

I grinned because I was walking up LeConte, up into the clouds once again.

Any aggravation left from the wild week or traffic jams flowed away faster than the waters of the West Prong of the Little Pigeon when I stopped at the trailhead. As soon as I saw the bridge across the stream, my mind traveled back to that first time my foot touched that bridge over 18 years ago. When I walked into the rhododendron thicket that borders the start of the trail, my heart silently sang a wordless tune.

Alum Cave is a fair trail, a just trail, one that travels five miles from U.S. 441 up to the summit of Mt. LeConte. Along the way, Alum takes hikers through the rhododendron thicket that's covered by a high canopy of hardwoods, up to an outcropping in a thicket of its own that opens to a view down the Sugarland Valley, then steepens as it passes Alum Cave Bluffs before ending in an evergreen grove on top of the mountain.

The trail's fairness and justice come from ample switchbacks and forgiving flat places along the way. The hard uphill parts are broken up by corners cut from the sides of the mountain – some of the corners stepping around to sheer drops that give a sense of wildness to the trail – so there are few, if any, long stretches that seem to go mercilessly upward forever as the hiker stares up the trail.

Yellows of every shape and shade dominated the color scheme on the lower part of the mountain with an evergreen background dotted by dollops of reds that lingered in some sections. The pace of fall seems uneven to me, with parts of the Smokies having already shed their summer growth while areas along Alum glittered like gold and swaths of color still cling to parts of the highlands.

Alum Cave Trail passes through Arch Rock 1.4 miles from the trailhead. The arch through the rock is narrow, the stone stairs that provide passage steep. In fact, the trip through Arch Rock feels more like passing through the eye of a needle than walking under an arch.

About three-quarters of a mile further on, the trail opens up with a view down the valley. Almost due north of this opening – the opening I walked up on those years ago that taught me there is a reward for hiking up the hard parts of the trail – a narrow rock ridge runs toward the top of LeConte. As the ridge rises from west to east, a hiker who knows where to look can see the real Needles Eye of LeConte.

A naturally formed opening in the shape of a circle stares back toward the trail. The eye of the needle never blinks and, for a good distance along the trail, it seems to maintain its circular shape, almost as if the eye is tracking my progress toward Alum Cave Bluffs. It is easy to imagine the eye as a mystical portal to another land, or an all-seeing eye watching over the land of the *shaconage*.

Not far past the Needles Eye, Alum Cave Bluffs juts out over the trail. Legend has it that this quarter-mile long gash in the mountain was mined for materials to make gunpowder during the Civil War. As I walked underneath the overhang of the Bluffs, I turned my camera skyward to get a shot of its height. Like every other time I've been here, it seems, drops of groundwater dripped from the edge of the cliff and splattered in my face. Fascinatingly, on the thin soil at the edge of the cliff, perhaps 80 feet above the trail, full-size trees and bushes grow out of the rock.

The trail past the Bluffs turns steeper and leaves behind the rhododendron thickets. Close to the summit, the path climbs out of the woodlands and makes its way along several rock faces. The safety-conscious Park Service has hooked thick wire cables to the mountain to give handholds to help hikers across sheer-rock sections of the trail. At a couple of places, the mountain drops off for hundreds of feet, making most any hiker at least stay close to the cables.

We brought a church group up to LeConte on a long-ago Good Friday. Weather set in early and a blustery rainstorm lashed the mountain as we made our way toward the top. As the wind whipped, gusts blew the storm so hard into the side of the mountain that the rain bounced off the sheer cliffs and flew upward, soaking us from below. My mother was along and just yesterday reminded me of when it rained upside down on the way to LeConte.

As I made my way up the back side of LeConte – Alum Cave Trail climbs the south side of the mountain, away from Gatlinburg and hidden from the valley – my mind wandered back to a section near the bottom of the trail. Several years ago, a severe storm hit LeConte and triggered a rockslide that wiped away parts of Alum Cave Trail. The trail was closed for an extended time, and the first time I was back on it after it reopened, I was stunned by the starkness. Rocks had come crashing down a fold in the mountain and leveled all vegetation as they fell. Nothing was visible but rock in that gully, all life seemingly buried forever or ripped up and carried away.

Today, though, as I rounded a turn and walked into that once obliterated area, greens and yellows and golds greeted me. Hardwood saplings were growing in the rocks, through the rocks, even on the rocks as fresh soil had washed down from above. New life had come to a once desolate place.

I think of the economic ruin that is concerning and consuming much of America right now. As companies go bankrupt and banks close and homeowners lose their homes, the economic landscape looks as desolate as it has in decades with some folks holding out little hope of the economy ever recovering. But, somewhere out there, with a little time, a little water and a little sun, growth will come again.

And, as I think of the healing that took place back down the mountain, I remember my first trip here, my heart a wasteland, ruined by a stormy relationship, rocked by the beginnings of a divorce, the love that had once grown obliterated by a deluge of problems and a cascade of difficulties.

I saw no way, as I struggled up Mt. LeConte in 1990 on my first trip here, that love would ever bud again, much less bloom, in the midst of the rock field my heart had become. Yet time passed, seasons changed and the hard soil of my heart softened as my relationship with Christ grew. As the living water and the light of the world, He turned my barren soul into a fertile field where love has grown again.

At the top of the Alum Cave Trail, a last stand of evergreens hangs on even though their nearby neighbors have fallen to the ravages of the adelgids. LeConte rolls out a welcome mat as Alum rewards the weary with an easy path lined with spruce and softened by moss-covered logs. A few flat yards, a right turn at the rocky trail intersection and a mere one-tenth of a mile further, and I'm back.

Back on Mt. LeConte.

Mt. LeConte
LeConte Lodge

The clouds never relented on LeConte today, actually wafting through the forest on top of the mountain and brushing by my legs. Retracing the now-familiar path to LeConte Lodge, I smiled as I descended the stairs of wood and grass that lead past the cabins and down to the dining room. I hung a left toward the office, stopped to read the new historical display and let myself acclimate to the altitude and my euphoric attitude.

It seems I always get giddy on LeConte. Most likely it's endorphins kicking in from the climb or a sensational surge from the sense of accomplishment. But the Lodge is a ruggedly romantic place that at once stirs the heart and seizes the soul and soothes the spirit. Though I know the Lodge is here and I've been here numerous times, to see the first buildings, to turn onto the stairs – even on a socked-in day like today – causes my heart to leap like I've suddenly come home.

I collected myself before I entered the office. No reason to, really. It's just that I've scared enough people with my winded and wild-eyed way on top of a mountain that I thought it best to spare the folks inside today. Though remodeled a bit, the wooden walls are still adorned with photos and news stories of other lovers of LeConte. The dominos and checkers are still on the tables or stacked beside the paperbacks on the bookshelves. Oil lamps are ready for when darkness falls since, thank goodness, electricity still hasn't made it to the guest areas of this mountaintop mecca.

My first trip here I had no idea what I'd find. I just walked up the mountain and sort of stumbled on the Lodge. I was stunned. In the middle of wilderness, on top of a mountain I'd seen (if I'd only looked) every day of my childhood, stood rows of wooden structures. No road, no tram, no trolley could get one here, the only access by foot by climbing a mountain.

The aura of LeConte is enhanced by its history. The second tallest mountain in the Great Smoky Mountains National Park at 6,593 feet, LeConte is named for John LeConte, a physicist from North Carolina who never set foot on the mountain. LeConte helped measure the mountain by monitoring barometers in his lab while others took readings on the mountain. Though a few feet shorter than Clingmans Dome, Mt. LeConte has the highest face in the Smokies, rising over one mile above its base in Gatlinburg, and, in fact, has the highest face east of the Mississippi.

A lodge, of sorts, has been on this site since 1925. As a park ranger told us after dinner tonight, a group called the Great Smoky Mountains Conservation Association started lobbying for protection of the Smokies after logging companies started stripping the mountains bare. Mt. LeConte was the most visible and viable site to showcase their cause, even though access was a hard day's hike up an undeveloped trail that passed by Rainbow Falls. The GSMCA commissioned a lodge here, and it was built in 1925 and 1926. As part of its lobbying effort, GSMCA brought local, state and national dignitaries to LeConte to give them a taste of the backcountry and to give the decision makers an up-close look at the mountains they were being asked to protect.

Not long after the lodge was built, Gatlinburg legend Jack Huff came to manage it. Huff loved LeConte, and a famous picture in the Lodge office shows Huff with a wooden chair strapped somewhat uncomfortably to his back, his mother sitting precariously in the chair as Huff carried her up the mountain. Another photo shows Huff astride Old Joe, his horse, in 1929 looking out from Clifftops. Old Joe was the first horse to climb LeConte.

There are photos of the legends of LeConte in the office as well. Grace McNicols of Maryville, Tennessee, made 244 round-trips to

LeConte, the last on her 92nd birthday. Paul Dinwiddie of Knoxville, Tennessee, hiked LeConte 750 times, more than any other hiker. But the grand dame of LeConte is the late Margaret Stevenson. Margaret came to LeConte 718 times, even though she didn't start climbing the mountain until she was in her 60s. Margaret also hiked all the 800-plus miles of trails in the Great Smoky Mountains National Park and her bronzed hiking boots occupy a place of honor in the Lodge office.

Though the history is intriguing and the atmosphere on top of LeConte exhilarating, a stay at the Lodge can become habit-forming. An old-fashioned family style dinner of soup, cornbread, beef, mashed potatoes, green beans and dessert of a peach and a melt-in-your mouth chocolate chip cookie refuels and refreshes guests after their climb. A bounteous breakfast the next morning stokes adventurers for the day ahead. The rustic accommodations – made somewhat exclusive by a rigorous reservation policy and overwhelming demand – transport the traveler back in time to simpler days and awaken the inner-Appalachian that, I'm convinced, still resides in many Americans.

That Appalachian spirit is one of discovery and self-sufficiency, one that finds joy in life's challenges – like walking up a mountain – and appreciates and embraces the ruggedness of the wilderness. Perhaps the wilderness awakens our own ruggedness, so often suppressed or depressed by modernity, and sparks that thing within us that sent many of our ancestors on a quest for a new land, a place where, by faith, courage, hard work and resourcefulness, they could pioneer a new and better life for themselves and those who came after them. Maybe that spark rekindles the fire of adventure in those who come to LeConte. It must. There was a twinkle in every eye around the dinner table tonight.

The Lodge lends itself to camaraderie, a slightly different type than the bonding in the backcountry, but an openness and gregariousness all the same. Tales are told of trails hiked to LeConte, stories of harsh weather and hard hikes are recounted and notes about timing of trips and gear needed are shared. Some have a favorite of the five trails that lead to the Lodge – Alum Cave, Boulevard, Bull Head, Rainbow Falls and Trillium Gap – while others like to try them all.

One couple at my table has come here every October for over 20 years. For another, this is their third trip. For some, though, once up LeConte is enough. But many folks love LeConte so much they renew their reservations year after year, even decade after decade. LeConte is intoxicating, to the point of becoming addictive.

For me, LeConte has become a touchstone, a place to come to gain perspective, to reorient myself, to reconnect with my Maker, to rekindle my inner-Appalachian. I've walked all the trails of this mountain that watched over me in my childhood, welcomed me home from college and wooed me when I became a wounded adult. On

LeConte's paths, I learned to live again after life crushed me nearly two decades ago.

Several years ago, I skipped work on my birthday and climbed LeConte, probably to prove I wasn't as old as the calendar said I was, but also to make another memory on the mountain. I was coming up either the Rainbow Falls Trail or Trillium Gap Trail, I can't remember which, when a sharp pain shot through my chest. It must have been a muscle spasm or heartburn or something, because it dissipated quickly. I thought for a nanosecond about turning back, but I continued to walk up LeConte. Pondering the unpleasant possibilities if the pain was something worse, I grinned to myself as I came to a fatalistic, though absolutely freeing conclusion. "It would be okay to die on this mountain," I thought, "because this is where I learned to live."

The winds are howling and the clouds climb across the mountain and race right by my door. The temperature is 28 degrees outside, but I am warm and happy and whole here on LeConte. I'm where I want to be. I'm where I need to be.

Mt. LeConte
Myrtle Point

The morning dawns with a crimson bridge stretching between mountaintops in the eastern sky. Crimson, rose, pink and orange stack above the Smokies before giving way to a sliver of gold beneath the faint blue of an awakening day. I'm shocked to be here. Last night's clouds were thick as soup on top of LeConte, and I held little hope they would clear by morning. My internal alarm clock missed my wakeup call by half an hour, leaving me in bed until 6:30 a.m.

Right now, though, night is slowly receding overhead, the moon above LeConte still making a stand though the coming sun is extinguishing the stars one by one. When I groggily looked out the door into the below-freezing day, a billion bursts of white burned in the blue-black night. I stumbled stupidly into my clothes, grabbed my gear and stepped out into the morning as Pigeon Forge glared its lights up at me from the valley with Sevierville's shine only slightly more muted.

The seven-tenths of a mile between the Lodge and Myrtle Point passed quickly. The trail sign pointing to Clifftops, the backcountry shelter and High Point were all but silhouettes as my torch-light bounced and bobbed along the trail while I coughed in the cold and my nose ran like a 5-year-old's. I dashed over the rocks, cursing my internal clock and mumbling, "Seven-tenths of a mile my rear." But, I'm here at the rock outcropping ringed with myrtle bushes before the sun winks awake in the east.

Morning on Myrtle Point. Dawn on the eastern end of LeConte. Sunrise in the Smokies. As I stand above the few clouds that dot the lowlands, the frigid wind rips across the denuded Fraser firs and wiggles the spruce I'm taking shelter behind. Sunrise promises to be sensational on this clear-as-a-bell morning.

Myrtle Point was nothing like this on my only other trip here for sunrise. On that Good Friday trip to LeConte with my church group, the mountain was covered by clouds when we awoke the next day. Ever the optimists (or seriously deluded), we made the walk in the dark from the lodge in hopes of getting a glimpse of the sunrise that was supposed to be so amazing.

Icy spots covered some of the rocks along the way from the Lodge and more than one of our group members took a tumble. But, we all made it to Myrtle in one piece and walked right into the cloud bank that clung hard to the mountain. Though disappointed, we held firmly to our agenda, a reading from the Psalms, I think, that contained a verse that said something about the sun.

At the estimated hour of sunrise, I read from the Psalm as we all wondered if we were sane since we'd walked in the dark to stare into a mist. I stood facing the crowd as they faced east and hurriedly read the passage while hoping the mutiny would wait until after breakfast. I glanced up at our group as I read the section about the sun to see if my friends were grinning, grimacing or glaring. Surprisingly, they were gaping.

"Keep reading," one of the guys shouted. I looked behind me and just as I had read about the sun, the clouds opened just enough for the sun to shine through. I returned to the Scripture and read some more, but the hole in the mist closed quickly, the sun now hidden. Still, we couldn't escape the feeling that God had winked at us through an opening in the clouds that day.

This morning's horizon has turned pastel with the blues and pinks calmer and quieter off in the eastern sky. The rains of two days ago cleared the air. Fog hangs low and the *shaconage* is real this morning rather than the human-made stuff that plagues the Smokies. Clingmans is greening with the dawn, lit by the mysterious rays that come even before the circle of the sun comes clear of the mountains in the distance.

In these last moments before the sun crests the horizon, I remember sunrises at Gethsemani, on Andrews Bald and the many other places – from Douglas Lake in Tennessee and Lone Mountain in Montana to Kauai in Hawaii, the Serengeti in Kenya and Mt. Kilimanjaro in Tanzania – I've greeted the day and collected a sunrise. There is a time, as light rises before the sun's golden arc appears above that distant line, when anticipation yields to a dint of doubt – foolishly, I'll admit – that day is going to dawn at all. But doubt always gives way to reality and a guessing game begins about where exactly on the horizon day will come.

It is here. Like that, the sun broke above the horizon just south of where my last guesstimate said it would show. An unencumbered golden globe peeked over the eastern end of the Smokies and the

Great Smoky Mountains National Park

mountains beyond. This is no lazy sunrise. Rather, the sun crested the horizon and climbed quickly as it illumined the mountains as if to suddenly shake the Smokies free from their slumber and the lethargy left over from a cloud-filled yesterday.

The sudden sunrise spills light along the ridgelines, making fabulously fast work of dawn and, in an instant, turns the mountains from black to purple to blue to green. The sideways sun softens the edges of the rugged places as it rousts the highest peaks first, then filters down to the valley to warm the world awake.

In this magic hour of morning, the new day dawned quickly, coming with a clarity I've seldom seen, bringing a day full of beauty, wonder and awe. The anticipation is over, all doubt erased about whether night would ever end. Day is here, a glorious, wonderful, hope-filled day started in the cold on top of LeConte. The kind of dawn, the kind of day, that pushes me forward with a new anticipation of what lies ahead now that night is gone.

Sanctuary

"How glorious a greeting the sun gives the mountains!"

John Muir

Mt. LeConte
Clifftops

From this vantage point, I once saw a thunderstorm walk across Blount County on legs of lightning, like a spider creeping across the valley with its eye on Thunderhead Mountain on the western end of the Smokies. I brought my son Reed and a couple of his friends here to Clifftops, only two-tenths of a mile southwest of LeConte Lodge, just after he turned 18 on a rite of passage of sorts. To mark his adulthood moment, I broke out cigars for us men to smoke on top of the mountain, the expanse of the Smokies beneath our feet, the world stretched out before us. We walked over to High Point, the tallest part of LeConte a little ways east of the Lodge, wrote down our dreams, shared them with each other and let the altitude and atmosphere convince us they might someday come true.

I'm back. Back on Clifftops, back where my love affair with LeConte began, back where I first put pen to page as I sat and stared at wave after wave of mountains rolling from the horizon before breaking against the base of LeConte and ebbing out into the valley. I missed the sunset here last night. Too many clouds and, truthfully, I was too cold and tired to even hazard a hope of seeing anything in the gloom. But, today has broken beautiful, and circumstance – or Providence – has sent me here to end this leg of my journey where I started it.

Visibility is at least 30 miles, maybe 50 – I'm not much of a judge of such things. Regardless, it's clear enough to see Clingmans Dome and the definition of the trees that top it. Down and south, I can catch the glint of windshields in the Newfound Gap parking lot. The fields of Cades Cove are visible, peeking out from behind the crests of mountains between here and there. Wears Valley, and maybe

Great Smoky Mountains National Park

Townsend, is filled with fog, a whitecap in an otherwise tranquil sea of grays and greens and reds. To the east, the mountains roll on and on, their ruggedness softened by the blue smoke of morning.

They say the mercury fell to 24 degrees here on LeConte last night. The winds still rush up from the valley, following the path of the predecessors that pushed the clouds away sometime in the night. They rush, then rest, then rush again before whispering to stillness, then repeating their cycle. This rocky crag feels cozy, comforting, consoling, even as it offers a view that leaves me awestruck.

Earlier, on Myrtle Point, the wind and cold ripped across the still awakening mountains and brought tears to my eyes. But the catch in my throat came from inside me instead of the outside atmosphere. Tears have welled again. The mountains move me. Particularly when I pause, when I stop from the artistic agenda and when I put away my hiking schedule. They move me with their beauty, and they move me with their blessings.

For that is what it is to see a sunrise, to gaze at mountaintops under a perfect blue sky on an October Sunday morning. It is a blessing. And, for all my faults, failures and foibles, this blessing has fallen on me. In my unworthiness, I sometimes weep at my good fortune. I am a blessed man to even once glimpse such magnificence, much less to be able to come back over and over again to the beauty of LeConte.

Sure, a geologic incident may have pushed these mountains up out of the earth, and the same winds that cool my neck right now are indeed capable of carrying seeds from somewhere else to be sown in the Smokies. But can beauty like this be a product of happenstance? I think not – no more than a Monet, a Rembrandt or a Van Gogh could have painted itself by an accidental spillage of splatters of paint on a canvas.

They say beauty is in the eye of the beholder, and I guess that's true. But, beauty abounds on mountaintops, down in the valley and everywhere around us. Too often, though, the beholder is blinded to it, careening through life with blinkered eyes that shut out the majesty that can be observed by the one whose eyes are open to it. Or, the beholder just may not be willing to go and see the beauty in the world around.

I used to say, "If you'll go where others won't, you'll see what others don't." I suppose that's still true. But, back then, when I first started coming to LeConte, to the Smokies, I wore that statement as a badge of pride, a point of superiority gained by grunting up mountainsides. And, yes, it is still true that if we desire to see the beauty in a world that is all too often cold and cruel and uncaring, we must go in search of it even if that means leaving behind the comforts of home and the coziness of the life we've created for ourselves.

Now, though, the statement saddens me. There are those who won't or don't care to go in search of the glory of Creation, even if it merely means taking a walk around their block or spending an afternoon in a park in the heart of a city. So many Americans are so programmed by modernity that they won't or don't step outside, breathe the real air, walk in the beauty of Creation and brush up against the Creator. Instead, they live every day in the artificiality of the world created by humans.

I'm saddened that some can't come to this glorious place – not just LeConte, but the whole of the Great Smoky Mountains – due to age or infirmity or ignorance of what the wild world holds for those who will come into it. This wild world helped me, healed me, changed me. It has, and will, do the same for others.

I have come back to my mountain, Mt. LeConte, where my own journey outside began. This mountain is my monastery, my place to pause, to pray, to think and walk closer with my God. This mountain is my muse, opening my soul and letting words and thoughts spill out, some that find the page, others that I hide in my heart. These mountains are my sanctuary, the place where I find serenity, security and safety.

When I first came to Clifftops those many years ago, my world was growing darker day by day, the gloom growing minute by minute. Those days are long past, and, most days, I walk in the light, and I've been blessed to climb higher than I ever could have imagined. As I walked back from sunrise on Myrtle Point this morning, I meditated on the suddenness of the sun's appearing. Deep inside me, a still small voice whispered, "A new day has dawned for you, too." What it holds, I do not know.

All I can do is walk toward it.

Sanctuary

Psalm of the Smokies

By J. Greg Johnson

Listen
Hear the earth
Groan and creak
Crack and thrust
The mountains skyward
From the surging sea
In an age before time.

Listen
To ten trillion raindrops
Patter on the peaks
Before gathering into streams
Then creeks, then rivers
That cut the crags and smooth the stones
Scattered by a marvelous act of God.

Listen
As the winds sigh
Along the ridgetops
Carrying the seeds
Of sanctuary
Divinely sowing
A half-million acres of heaven on earth.

Listen
To the native voices
Coaxing the land
To share its life
Cultivating a culture
Wise and strong and proud
Long before the white man came.

Sanctuary

Listen
To their tears on the trail
As they trudge
From their home
Toward misery and nothing
But too many graves
Under orders of mean and misguided men.

Listen
To the wagon rumble
The banjo twang
The fiddle whine
The preacher pray
As chinked chimneys send smoke
Through the coves and across the valleys.

Listen
To the saws sing
The axes swing
The trees wail
As the oldest fall
And the railroad chugs
While the mountains moan
As what was is lost for logs.

Listen
Hear cars come
And voices gather
To speak of commerce
And conservation, profit
And preservation
As an inkling of an idea
Forms in the people.

Listen
To the words of Chapman and Davis
The heart of Kephart
From the Back of Beyond
And the money of Rockefeller
That speaks the language
The loggers understand.

Listen
To the families of farmers
Being told they must go
And the cries of the children
As they flee to flatter lands
Leaving Grandma and Grandpa
Alone in the cold dark ground
On the side of a mountain.

Listen
To the shovels and picks
And hammers and men
Of that Depression time
As they carve trails
Build roads and stack stones
For the permanent enjoyment of the people.

Listen
As millions now come
To glimpse the glory
Of a place preserved
And honored
And loved
By a nation in need of wilderness.

Listen
To the high country mourn
As the firs fall silent
Sapped of life

Sanctuary

While hemlocks hurt
As the adelgids bore
And cause them to cry.

Listen
To Cammerer and Gregory
Davenport and Fontana
Thunderhead and Clingmans
LeConte and the Chimneys
Deep Creek and Sugarlands
Cataloochee and Cades Cove
Sing the siren song.

Listen
As the balds and bunions
Beckon the brave
The valleys and vistas
Call the courageous
The paths and peaks
Woo those who wander.

Listen
As the winds whip
Across the crest
Brushing blush the cheeks
Of the hikers and the hurried
The frazzled and the worried
Who find peace in the wild.

Listen
To the psalm of the Smokies
A symphony of praise
For the pinnacle of Creation
A melody of the mountains
That stirs hearts
Soothes souls
And inspires all who enter.

Finding Sanctuary

(Distances are approximate. Hiking time does not allow for time to sit and stare and think and write and take photos. Hiking time based on two miles per hour. For detailed trail information and descriptions, I recommend "Hiking Trails of the Smokies" published by the Great Smoky Mountains Association.)

Abrams Falls
    Trailhead: Take Laurel Creek Road to Cades Cove. Sign for Abrams Falls Trail is on right almost half way around Cades Cove Loop.
    Distance: 5 miles roundtrip
    Hiking time: 2 ½ to 3 ½ hours
    Difficulty: Easy to moderate with uphill in middle of hike

Albright Grove
    Trailhead: Take U.S. 321 for 15.5 miles from Gatlinburg to Baxter Road on right. Sign for Maddron Bald Trail is on right on Baxter Road. Park Service gate marks start of Maddron Bald Trail. Parking is available at the gate and just around turn. Follow Maddron Bald Trail to Albright Grove Loop.
    Distance: Approximately 7 miles roundtrip
    Hiking Time: 3 ½ to 4 ½ hours
    Difficulty: Moderate to hard in a few sections

Andrews Bald
    Trailhead: Take U.S. 441 to Clingmans Dome. Andrews Bald is reached by the Forney Ridge Trail which leaves from the Clingmans Dome parking.
    Distance: 3.6 miles roundtrip
    Hiking time: Approximately 1 ½ to 2 hours
    Difficulty: Moderate mainly because of rocky trail near the trailhead

Baskins Creek
> Trailhead: From Gatlinburg, take Cherokee Orchard Road to Roaring Fork Motor Nature Trail. (Don't turn onto Roaring Fork!) There's a parking space on the left where Roaring Fork Motor Nature Trail turns right. Walk about ¼ mile up Roaring Fork Motor Nature Trail. Baskins Creek Trail leaves from the left. (To retrace the hike described in this book, leave a second vehicle near the end of Baskins Creek Road at the national park boundary sign.)
> Distance: 1.5 miles to Baskins Creek Falls. The cemetery is about 0.5 miles before you reach the falls. The cemetery is marked by a trail sign. The trail to the falls doesn't have a sign but is clearly defined. If you return to your car on Cherokee Orchard Road, total distance is about 3.0 miles. If you take my route, the walk to Baskins Creek Road is approximately 2 miles past the falls for a total of about 3.5 miles.
> Hiking time: 1 ½ to 2 hours
> Difficulty: Easy downhill from the trailhead. Easy walk down to Baskins Creek Road. Moderate uphill if you return to Cherokee Orchard Road.

Cades Cove
> Trailhead: Take Laurel Creek Road from Townsend Y.
> Distance: None
> Hiking time: None
> Difficulty: Easy

Charlies Bunion
> Trailhead: Take U.S. 441 to Newfound Gap. Take the Appalachian Trail from eastern end of the Newfound Gap parking lot.
> Distance: 8 miles roundtrip
> Hiking time: 4 to 5 hours

Difficulty: Moderate to hard with uphill climb up Mt. Kephardt. DANGER: Rocks at the Bunion slippery when wet and sheer drops around the Bunion.

Chimney Tops

Trailhead: Take U.S. 441. Signs mark the trailhead about 7 miles south of Gatlinburg.

Distance: 4 miles roundtrip

Hiking time: 2 to 3 hours

Difficulty: Strenuous with constant incline on the way up. DANGER: Rocks at top slippery when wet.

Clingmans Dome

Trailhead: Take U.S. 441 to Clingmans Dome. Trail leaves from western end of parking lot.

Distance: 1.0 miles roundtrip

Hiking time: Approximately 1 to 1 ½ hours

Difficulty: Easy to moderate. The paved trail is steep.

Gregory Bald

Trailhead: From Cades Cove entrance gate, take Cades Cove Loop to Cable Mill area. Turn right off the Loop just past entrance to Cable Mill and follow signs to Parsons Branch Road. Turn right on Parsons Branch Road (one-way, rugged road) for a couple of miles to graveled parking lot on right. Gregory Bald Trail leaves from eastern (left) side of road. (Hannah Mountain Trail leaves on western side of road.)

Distance: Approximately 10 miles roundtrip.

Hiking time: 5 to 7 hours

Difficulty: Moderate to hard; steep uphill near Bald

Grotto Falls

Trailhead: From Gatlinburg, take Cherokee Orchard Road to Roaring Fork Motor Nature Trail. Turn right onto Roaring Fork Motor Nature Trail. Signs mark the Trillium Gap trailhead. Grotto Falls is on Trillium Gap Trail.

Distance: 2.8 miles roundtrip
Hiking time: 1 ½ to 2 ½ hours
Difficulty: Moderate with steady incline on way to falls.

Laurel Falls
Trailhead: Take Laurel Creek Road from Sugarlands Visitor Center. Sign marks trailhead on right.
Distance: 2.6 miles roundtrip
Hiking time: 1 ½ to 2 ½ hours
Difficulty: Easy. Trail is paved but often crowded in spring, summer and fall.

Little Greenbrier Schoolhouse
Trailhead: From Pigeon Forge, take U.S. 321 to Wears Valley. Turn left onto Lyons Springs Road to Wear Cove entrance to Park. Turn left at sign for Little Greenbrier Schoolhouse just after entering Park. From Gatlinburg, take U.S. 441 to Little River Road. Turn right on Little River Road. Turn right at Metcalf Bottoms Campground. Turn right at sign for Little Greenbrier Schoolhouse.
Distance: None
Hiking time: None
Difficulty: Easy

Mt. Cammerer
Trailhead: Take U.S. 321 to sign for Cosby Campground. Sign in campground points to hiker parking. Low Gap Trail leaves from hiker parking lot. Take Low Gap Trail for 2.9 miles to Appalachian Trail. Turn east on AT for 2.1 miles to Mt. Cammerer Trail. Mt. Cammerer Lookout is 0.6 miles from AT on Mt. Cammerer Trail.
Distance: 11.2 miles roundtrip
Hiking time: 5 ½ to 7 ½ hours
Difficulty: Hard to strenuous on Low Gap Trail. Moderate to hard on AT. Moderate on Mt. Cammerer Trail.

Mt. Collins Shelter
> Trailhead: Take Clingmans Dome Road from U.S. 441 to sign for Fork Ridge Trail on left. A sign across road from Fork Ridge Trail points to Appalachian Trail. Walk west on AT for about a quarter mile to pick up Sugarland Mountain Trail. Take Sugarland Mountain Trail another quarter mile or so to Mt. Collins Shelter.
> Distance: Approximately 1.5 miles roundtrip
> Hiking time: ¾ to 1 ¼ hours
> Difficulty: Easy to moderate

Mt. LeConte: Alum Cave Trail
> Trailhead: Take U.S. 441 from Sugarlands Visitor Center about 8.6 miles. Signs mark trailhead on the left.
> Distance: 10 miles roundtrip to summit of Mt. LeConte and LeConte Lodge. (Arch Rock is 1.4 miles from trailhead. Needles Eye is approximately 2.0 miles from trailhead. Alum Cave Bluffs are 2.3 miles from trailhead.)
> Hiking time: 5 to 7 hours
> Difficulty: Moderate to hard for most of trail. Hard to strenuous section around Alum Cave Bluffs. Steep drop-offs in sections and some sections of trail are rock.

Mt. LeConte: Clifftops
> Trailhead: Follow signs from LeConte Lodge to Clifftops.
> Distance: 0.5 miles roundtrip from LeConte Lodge
> Hiking time: ½ to ¾ hours
> Difficulty: Moderate with rocky sections

Mt. LeConte: LeConte Lodge (see Alum Cave Trail)

Mt. LeConte: Myrtle Point
> Trailhead: Follow signs from LeConte Lodge to Myrtle Point.
> Distance: 1.4 miles roundtrip from LeConte Lodge
> Hiking time: ¾ to 1 ¼ hours
> Difficulty: Moderate with rocky sections

Newfound Gap
> Trailhead: Take U.S. 441 to top of Great Smoky Mountains National Park.
> Distance: None
> Hiking time: None
> Difficulty: Easy

Porters Creek
> Trailhead: Take U.S. 321 from Gatlinburg to Pittman Center. Turn right into Greenbrier section of National Park. Follow signs to Porters Creek trailhead.
> Distance: 2.0 miles roundtrip to Smoky Mountain Hiking Club Cabin
> Hiking time: 1 to 1 ½ hours
> Difficulty: Easy. Trail is gravel road to cabin area.

Rainbow Falls
> Trailhead: From Gatlinburg, take Cherokee Orchard Road to sign for Rainbow Falls Trail.
> Distance: 5.8 miles roundtrip
> Hiking time: 3 to 4 hours
> Difficulty: Moderate to hard in some rocky sections

Ramsey Cascades
> Trailhead: Take U.S. 321 from Gatlinburg to Pittman Center. Turn right into Greenbrier section of National Park. Follow signs to Ramsey Cascades trailhead.
> Distance: 8 miles roundtrip
> Hiking time: 4 to 6 hours
> Difficulty: Hard to strenuous with last half mile strenuous.

Rocky Top
> Trailhead: (My route in "Sanctuary" combined Rocky Top, Thunderhead and Spence Field.) Take Laurel Creek Road toward Cades Cove. Lead Cove Trail leaves from south side of Laurel Creek Road. Lead Cove Trail intersects with Bote

Mountain Trail at 1.8 miles. Bote Mountain intersects with Appalachian Trail at Spence Field at 2.9 miles. Rocky Top is approximately 1.25 miles east of Spence Field on Appalachian Trail.

Distance: Approximately 12 miles roundtrip

Hiking time: 6 to 8 hours

Difficulty: Lead Cove and Bote Mountain are moderate to hard. Section on AT to Rocky Top is hard to strenuous.

Spence Field

Trailhead: (My route in "Sanctuary" combined Rocky Top, Thunderhead and Spence Field.) Take Laurel Creek Road toward Cades Cove. Lead Cove Trail leaves from south side of Laurel Creek Road. Lead Cove Trail intersects with Bote Mountain Trail at 1.8 miles. Bote Mountain intersects with Appalachian Trail at Spence Field at 2.9 miles.

Distance: Approximately 10 miles roundtrip

Hiking time: 5 to 7 hours

Difficulty: Lead Cove and Bote Mountain are moderate to hard.

Sugarlands Quiet Walkway

Trailhead: On U.S. 441, just past Sugarlands Vistor Center. This is the second walkway driving south, across road from Huskey Gap Trail sign.

Distance: Approximately 1 mile roundtrip

Hiking time: 30 to 45 minutes

Difficulty: Easy

The Jump Off

Trailhead: Take U.S. 441 to Newfound Gap. Take the Appalachian Trail from eastern end of Newfound Gap parking lot. At 2.7 miles, turn onto Boulevard Trail for less than half a mile. Trail to the Jump Off leaves to right for 0.5 mile hike to Jump Off.

Distance: Approximately 7 miles roundtrip
Hiking time: 3 ½ to 4 ½ hours
Difficulty: Appalachian Trail section is moderate to hard. Trail from Boulevard to Jump Off is rocky and ragged.

Thunderhead Mountain
Trailhead: (My route combined Rocky Top, Thunderhead and Spence Field.) Take Laurel Creek Road toward Cades Cove. Lead Cove Trail leaves from south side of Laurel Creek Road. Lead Cove Trail intersects with Bote Mountain Trail at 1.8 miles. Bote Mountain intersects with Appalachian Trail at Spence Field at 2.9 miles. Thunderhead is approximately 1.75 miles east of Spence Field on Appalachian Trail.
Distance: Approximately 13 miles roundtrip
Hiking time: 7 to 9 hours
Difficulty: Lead Cove and Bote Mountain are moderate to hard. Section on AT to Thunderhead is hard to strenuous.

Walker Sisters Cabin
Trailhead: From Pigeon Forge, take U.S. 321 to Wears Valley. Turn left onto Lyons Springs Road to Wear Cove entrance to Park. Turn left at sign for Little Greenbrier Schoolhouse just after entering Park. From Gatlinburg, take U.S. 441 to Little River Road. Turn right on Little River Road. Turn right at Metcalf Bottoms Campground. Turn right at sign for Little Greenbrier Schoolhouse. Trail leaves from parking lot.
Distance: 2.2 miles roundtrip
Hiking time: 1 to 1 ½ hours
Difficulty: Easy with gentle grade on gravel road.

Great Smoky Mountains National Park

Sanctuary Rated

(Hikes in this book rated by difficulty.)

Easy walks (less than 3 miles)
    Newfound Gap
    Cades Cove
    Little Greenbrier Schoolhouse
    Sugarlands Quiet Walkway
    Clingmans Dome
    Walker Sisters Cabin
    Laurel Falls
    Porters Creek
    Mt. Collins Shelter

Moderate walks (less than 5 miles)
    Grotto Falls
    Andrews Bald
    Abrams Falls
    Baskins Creek
    Chimney Tops (steep)

Hard walks (less than 10 miles)
    Rainbow Falls
    The Jump Off
    Albright Grove
    Charlies Bunion
    Ramsey Cascades
    Gregory Bald
    Spence Field

Difficult hikes (over 10 miles)
    Mt. LeConte (via Alum Cave Trail, includes LeConte Lodge, Myrtle Point and Clifftops)
    Rocky Top
    Mt. Cammerer
    Thunderhead Mountain

About the Author

A native of East Tennessee, Greg Johnson grew up in the shadows of the Great Smoky Mountains. His heart dances when he hears a banjo twang or a fiddle whine. Greg's sometimes stirring, sometimes sarcastic, sometimes searing, occasionally entertaining opinion columns appear weekly in the Knoxville (Tenn.) News Sentinel. He and his wife Diane live and write in Sevier County, Tenn.

Contact info:
By mail:
    Greg Johnson
    P.O. Box 1333
    Pigeon Forge, TN 37863

By e-mail:
    jgregjohnson@hotmail.com

Made in the USA
San Bernardino, CA
16 September 2014